COLLEGE AUDITION

WORKBOOK

A step-by-step guide through the College Audition process

Written By:

Dave Clemmons, Michelle Evans, Holly Garmon, Camiah Mingorance & Pat Valleroy

www.collegeauditionproject.com

Published by College Audition Project

www.collegeauditionproject.com

Copyright © 2019

Dave Clemmons, Michelle Evans, Holly Garmon, Camiah Mingorance & Pat Valleroy

For our amazing families, students, friends, and colleagues that have supported us through this crazy process. We owe a part of this to each one of you and could not have done it without you all!

To all of our CAP Families, thank you for letting us be a part of your journey. You are truly family and we are so excited to see where this exciting path will lead. We are always here to be a soft place to land!

WORKBOOK INDEX

Introduction...5

Our Story...6

Chapter 1: Selecting Your Schools...7-16

Chapter 2: The Application Process...17-32

Chapter 3: Knowing Your Type...33-37

Chapter 4: How To Pick The Right Material.....................................38-68

Chapter 5: Prescreens...69-79

Chapter 6: Live Auditions & Unifieds...80-94

Chapter 7: After The Audition..95-103

Chapter 8: Getting Ready For College..104-106

List of Schools...107-110

Overused Material...111-117

College Audition Project...118-121

Biographies...122-126

Introduction

We are so excited that you have this workbook in front of you right now. We have put over a decade of hands on training into this workbook so that we can help YOU through this complicated process. We hope that you will find the CAP Workbook a comfort and aid.

This book is intended to be written in, highlighted, dog-eared and used. We don't want you to add this to your bookshelf, we intended this book to be carried with you, shoved in your bag and pulled out in your times of need. In our opinion, if by the end of your audition season the cover is torn and the words on the page are barely recognizable, then we have done our job in creating a tool that you can USE!

If while you are going through this book you feel that you could use more help or assistance, we urge you to register online for our CAP website and the Navigator. The Navigator will take everything you love about this book and transform it into a digital medium that you can use on the go. We even have an app you can download on all your devices! The Navigator is also home to a college database, where you can add schools, set reminders about deadlines and auditions, store media and so much more. No need for those spreadsheets and planners anymore, the CAP Navigator will take care of all of that for you. Also, access to students accounts is included with every package for parents, teachers and non- CAP coaches!

Again, we are so excited to be a part of your journey and hope that the content found in these pages will help take some of the stress out of this process!

Best Wishes,

The CAP Team

Our Story

Our story starts near Atlanta at a performing arts studio called *The Performer's Warehouse* where the five Co-Owners met while working together. It was there that the team realized that all of the previous expertise and training in their specific field made them an unstoppable team, and thus CAP was founded. The five Co-Founders and Owners are Camiah Mingorance of *CEM Music Studios*, Dave Clemmons of *DCCAP,* Holly Garmon of *The Performer's Warehouse*, Michelle Evans of *MJE Acting Studio,* and Pat Valleroy with *Emerging Artists*.

Individually the CAP team members have had their own successes and careers in the performing arts, each member with a separate focus and training. It is these differences that make our team so special. CAP is not just one person trying to juggle everything. With CAP you get the knowledge and experience of 5 individuals with different skill sets. While we all manage our own careers and businesses, we always know we do some of our *BEST* work when we combine our knowledge to coach students and help parents through this complicated process.

After helping students and parents through college auditions for the last decade, we knew that we could make the process easier. We slowly started putting our tips, experience, and knowledge on paper, saying that one day we would write a book. In 2018, feeling that the need for a digital outlet for families going through the college audition process was more pressing, we decided to officially create CAP and the CAP Navigator. We took everything that we had been putting on paper, turned it over to a web developer and thus CAP was born!

Now, after the success of our website and online tools, we are putting everything back on paper so that even more families can have access to CAP. However, we also noticed that, while there were traditional books about the college audition process, there were not really workbooks that could help a student through the process. So, the CAP Workbook was created...just for YOU!

Chapter One

SELECTING YOUR SCHOOLS

HOW TO RESEARCH SCHOOLS

Making a list of schools can be a difficult endeavor. It is important to think about many factors when choosing your schools. You need to know what type of a degree you want, what part of the country you want to be in, if you fit the school's academic requirements, if the curriculum fits your particular needs, if it's the right fit for you and most importantly, do the financial costs fit your budget?

Many people are tempted to visit schools up front, but it might be more effective to visit specific campuses once you know which schools have accepted you. If you want to get a feel for the different types and sizes of schools, we suggest visiting campuses that are in your area during a vacation or school holiday. Each state has similar schools that you can visit affordably and will give you the same understanding of size and type of campus.

What to look for in choosing your schools:

Academics:

1. What is the average GPA of accepted students? Do you meet or exceed this?

2. What is the average SAT/ACT score of accepted students? Do you meet or exceed this?

3. Have you successfully completed the required number of Math, Science and Language courses for entrance into the college or university?

Financial:

1. What are the application fees for each school?

2. What is the annual tuition for the school?

3. How much is room and board per year?

4. Are there any additional fees associated with attending the school and when are they assessed?

5. What kind of travel is involved for you to get to and from the school? What kind of costs will be associated with the travel?

6. What kind of scholarships would you likely be awarded to attend the college?

Location:

1. How far away is the school from your home?

2. Consider the ease/difficulty of travelling to and from the school.

3. What is the weather like where the school is located?

School Size:

1. Is the school a Conservatory within a larger university?

2. Is the school itself a large university?

3. Is it a mid-size college or university?

4. Is it a small college, arts school, conservatory or liberal arts college?

Type of Degrees offered:

BFA (Bachelor of Fine Arts) Degree

BA (Bachelor of Arts) Degree

BM (Bachelor of Music) Degree

A Bachelor of Arts degree will require more general education credits compared to a Bachelor of Fine Arts where the main focus is intensive study of the arts and less academic course requirements. With a BA degree, generally 40% of credits are within the study of your major, and with a BFA degree, credits are generally 75% within your major.

Choosing between the two degrees really depends on the student's career goals and learning styles. Students who are eager to have more academic courses may want to consider looking for a BA program or a university program. Those students who want to focus on intensive arts training for four years without the additional academic credit requirements may want to look for the BFA or conservatory program. Neither choice is wrong. A student can get everything they need from either program/degree type as long as they are completely devoted to their studies. Basically, you will get out of a program what you put into the program, so put your very best into whatever program you attend.

BM (Bachelor of Music) Degree
A Bachelor of Music degree will function a lot like a BFA program, however instead of the program being housed under the Department of Theatre it is housed under the Department of Music. So, don't let the "M" deter you from pursuing this degree option. There are some very popular musical theatre programs that offer a BM instead of a BFA. Oklahoma City University and Baldwin Wallace University are two good examples.

Curriculum:

1. What kind of academics will you be required to take in order to graduate? How many credits of Science, Math, Language, English/Composition and/or Humanities are necessary?

2. What kind of Acting classes will you receive? Will you be given a firm base in Technique, Movement, Voice, Accents, Stage Combat, etc.?

3. What kind of Dance classes will be offered and how often will you attend them? Look for classes offered in Ballet, Jazz, Modern Dance, Tap, Partnering, Choreography, and Musical Theatre. Are these classes leveled? How are they graded?

4. What sort of Voice Training/Singing classes will you have access to? Will you be assigned a voice coach? If so, what is your responsibility cost-wise? Does the school offer training in Music Theory, Sight Reading, Key Board Training, Vocal Instruction and/or Musical Theatre Repertoire?

5. What Master Classes will be available to you? Who are the classes taught by and how often are they offered in an academic year?

Graduation and Life Prep Classes:

1. Does the school offer Summer Programs, Study Abroad opportunities and/or Internships in your area of study?

2. Are there courses offered in Preparing for Agents and Management and/or Preparing for Professional Auditioning?

Faculty:

1. Where did the faculty members receive their training?

2. What are their professional credits?

3. Does the faculty perform and/or study during the summer breaks?

4. What theatres and groups are the faculty members associated with in the community and beyond?

5. Will you be taught by Grad students? Visiting Professors? Associate Professors?

Alumni:

1. Are the alumni working in their field of concentration since graduation? What is the percentage of graduates that are employed?

2. Where have the alumni worked since graduation and in what media (Broadway, movies, TV, Cruise Ships, etc.)?

Performance Session:

1. How many shows a year does the school produce? Who directs them?

2. When can you audition for these shows? Some schools do not allow freshman to audition.

3. Do they have student-run productions? How many per year?

4. Are students allowed to cross-over between Theatre, Musical Theatre, Dance and Voice shows and concerts?

5. What is the school's policy on returning to school after leaving for professional opportunities outside of the school? Is it allowed?

6. Is it possible to double major (or minor) in Musical Theatre, Theatre, Dance or Voice with another academic concentration (Education or business for example)? If so, will you need to stay an extra year to complete the requirements?

7. Will you be auditioning for productions against Grad students?

Opportunities within the Community:

1. Are there LORT/Equity Theatres in the area?

2. Will you be permitted to audition for their productions when not cast in the school's show?

3. Will you be permitted to accumulate Equity points for these outside opportunities?

Other Opportunities to Consider:

1. Does the school offer Fraternities and Sororities?

2. What other clubs and social experiences might you participate in?

3. Are there leadership opportunities and Honor Societies you can earn membership in?

4. Does the school offer intercollegiate sports programs and intramurals?

All these aspects should be thoroughly researched to determine the schools that best fit YOUR needs. Do not allow yourself to be sidetracked by the prestige of the school. If you would like more detailed help on choosing your list just schedule a consultation with any of our college specialists.

WORKSHEET A
SCHOOL SELECTION

1. What kind of college setting would be right for you?

2. With what you know now, would you prefer (Circle All that Apply):

   University   College   Conservatory within a University   No Preference

3. Degree you are interested in working for (Circle all that apply):

   BFA in Musical Theatre   BA in Musical Theatre   BFA in Acting

   BA in Acting/Dramatic Arts   BA Theatre Arts   BM in Musical Theatre

4. Do you plan on pursuing a minor or double major?

   If so what would you minor/double major in?

5. What size school do you want to attend (circle all that apply):

   Large   Medium   Small   Not Sure

6. Is location important? Describe what you would like and any areas or climates you do not want to live in while attending school.

7. Is there a particular focus in the program that is important to you:

   Strong Vocal/Music   Strong Dance   Strong Acting

8. In order of your greatest strength to weakest, circle what you would describe as your skill level:

   Dancer/Singer/Actor   Dancer/Actor/Singer   Singer/Dancer/Actor

   Singer/Actor/Dancer   Actor/Singer/Dancer   Actor/Dancer/Singer

9. Do you have a financial limit for tuition and Room & Board? What is the most you can spend?

   Remember that there is more cost besides tuition and Room & Board:

10. What is your current GPA?

11. Have you taken the SAT/ACT?

    What are your scores?
    Do you plan on taking them again?

12. Approximately how many schools do you plan on auditioning for?

13. Will you be auditioning in the fall for early decision spots? Where?

14. Is a school with a Senior Showcase important to you?

15. Do you want a school that will allow for extra activities, such as: Honors College, religious clubs, sports, sororities/fraternities, leadership work, community service? If so, please list all that are important to you.

16. Describe your personality: are you someone who thrives in a smaller, close-knit supportive environment? Or do you improve and flourish in a competitive rigorous environment?

Need Help Selecting Schools?
Get a consult with a CAP Coach!

Chapter Two

APPLYING TO SCHOOLS

APPLICATION PROCESS

College applications are a multi-step process. They are expensive and time consuming. Make sure you have a working budget with your parents so you both know what to expect!

1. Take the ACT and SAT. We suggest taking both, as they are very different tests. You should plan on taking both tests a minimum of two times during your JUNIOR year.
2. Pick your 15-20 schools. Be aware that this list will change many times during the year.
3. Begin work on your essays. These should be prepared during the early to mid-summer before your SENIOR year.
4. Start the applications. Begin as soon as they are available, which is usually early August. DO NOT wait on this. There is no time for this during your Senior year. This is a HUGE mistake that many students make and it adds unnecessary pressure to a very stressful time!
5. Every school charges an application fee. Be prepared and add this to your budget. This can very easily get out of hand. Most are around $35-50. These are paid when you send in the application.

6. Be pro-active and check to make sure the applications go through and that the schools have everything they need to make a decision. This is your responsibility. They will not come to you if something isn't finished.
7. You will have to have ACT/SAT scores sent in to each school, as well as your high school transcripts. There are fees for this as well, so make sure you know what the charges are to add to your budget.
8. Be prepared to add several schools as the year progresses. There will be schools that you will add as you fine tune your college package and your list changes. There will be schools that you audition for at CAP United Auditions or National Unifieds that you will need to apply for if you like them or they request you to do so. If your essays are done, you can turn these around quickly.

By the time Senior year starts, your college applications should be completed to the best of your ability. This will qualify you for early admittance into many schools. As you add new schools, you will be able to finish the new applications with limited time. Be aware that each college also charges an audition fee. These are usually between $25-80. Make sure you add this to your budget for the year. Communicate with your parents so there are no surprises and this process will be easier.

After you have applied to the school, you need to apply to audition for the theatre program. Some schools will want you to wait until you have been accepted, some will want you to pass the pre-screen first, and some will want you to apply right away.

Once you have completed your application, go to the theatre page and look for their application process. If you are a CAP student you can access this information in the College Database. Each school will have a 1-2-page application. Once you have finished the application, you will be able to submit your rec letters, headshot, resume, essays, etc. You will not be able to schedule your audition until this is done, so do not wait until the last minute. The quicker this is done, the quicker you can lay out your schedule for the audition season!

ESSAYS

Almost every school that you apply to will want an essay of some sort. Some schools will want more than one. Some schools want essays several pages long, and some want paragraph answers. Because your senior year is so stressful and busy, we suggest preparing your essays the summer before your senior year.

Most schools will provide you with a few topics for your essay. Common themes are: Why do you want to attend our school? What do you see in your future? Tell us about you, and why we should choose you?

In all instances, they are seeking to get to know YOU. They receive thousands of applications, and they are trying to determine who best fits their school environment. It is very important to be honest in these essays. They want to know the real you. They are not looking for perfect essays. You need to show them who you are as a person and how you will fit into their program.

Once you select your topic, take a day or two to really think about what they are asking. Do an outline with points you want to make. Write your first draft and let a teacher or mentor look at it. Do not be tempted to make up false sob stories, or to try and impress them. Just be you and know that is enough.

We suggest writing a basic essay on all the topics above and edit them to fit the schools you choose. Don't wait until October or November to begin this. You need to have your applications turned in and all documents sent to each school at the earliest possible date. Remember, you are much more likely to get accepted early, than later in the year.

SUBMITTING DOCUMENTATION

You will need to send your test scores, your academic transcripts, and your academic letters of recommendation to every school for which you are applying. This can get quite costly. It is best to send these as soon as your application has been sent to the school, as this will lead to quick academic acceptances and the best chance at scholarships based on grades. The steps below will make this process smoother:

1. At the beginning of the school year visit your advisor's office and ask them what kind of envelopes they prefer for sending transcripts. Some high schools require a fee for sending or providing transcripts and they take care of everything else. Other schools may ask you to provide white, manila or possibly another kind of envelope. You want to make sure you have exactly what they require so you can fast track this process as much as possible!
2. Make sure you have the correct addresses for each school you need to send a transcript, and you know what department the information should be sent to.
3. If your school sends electronically, make sure you have the correct email address for the department to which the transcript should be sent.
4. Be prepared for a small charge from your school. The charge is usually between $3-$10 per school.
5. Schedule a meeting with your counselor for academic letters of recommendation in August/September.
6. Give them a list of your accomplishments, awards, academic grades, volunteer work, extra-curricular activities, hobbies, etc.
7. Ask your favorite teachers for recommendations also. Give your teacher the same list you gave your counselor.
8. You will need to bring stamped envelopes for your teachers with the address of each school on them.

9. If recommendation letters can send electronically, make sure you follow up to see that they have been sent. Remember we all get busy, and your teachers might forget. It is your responsibility to make sure it has been completed.

10. Be certain to write a quick Thank You note to any teachers, or community members, who write a recommendation for you.

Your test scores will be sent by the SAT and ACT testing programs. Each time you take the test, you are allowed several free schools. If you take the test more than once, change the college each time so you don't have to pay for every school.

THE SUPERSCORE

Some schools that you will apply to may ask you to list your best score and the date of the exam and then calculate a composite or a superscore.

How to calculate your superscore:

ACT Superscore: The average of your highest Science, Math Reading and English scores

SAT Superscore: The sum of your highest Evidence-Based Reading, Writing and Math scores.

You will need to find out the policy for each school and see if they accept will accept a super score. Some schools may even recommend that you submit all scores available, that way they can consider you for scholarships, honors programs or others.

MANAGING COMMUNICATION

You will begin to receive a lot of emails from various sources such as academic offices, financial aid offices, the Fine Arts departments, etc. There are few things you should consider before an important email goes unread or lost altogether.

1. Create an email address that is strictly for college auditions. This will be the email that you give to everyone related to this process. You will know when you receive an email at that address that it needs your attention and it is less likely to get lost amongst dozens of junk emails. You may want to keep this email as your professional email, so don't make the email a joke. This is also the email that will be listed on your resume.

2. Check your email on a daily basis! Many times, you will need to respond within a time limit and you don't want to miss a deadline.

3. If you're not sure how to respond to an email or whether a response is even required, ask a trusted adult - a parent, a teacher or a CAP professional. Let them help you word a reply so that you present a professional demeanor to everyone you come in contact with.

```
┌─────────────────────────────────────────────────────────────────┐
│        WHICH E-MAIL ARE YOU USING FOR YOUR COLLEGE AUDITION PROCESS? │
│                                                                   │
│                                                                   │
│        _____       │
│                                                                   │
│                WHAT PASSWORD ARE YOU USING?                       │
│                                                                   │
│                                                                   │
│        _____       │
└─────────────────────────────────────────────────────────────────┘
```

DID YOU KNOW….

The CAP website has a place to store all of your college audition related passwords?

LETTERS OF RECOMMENDATION

You will need academic letters of recommendation, which we covered in Submitting Documents. However, you will also need theatre letters of recommendation. We suggest you ask for a letter from your acting teacher, your dance teacher, and your vocal teacher. These letters need to be requested as early as possible. Your teachers will need AT LEAST two weeks to get these letters completed.

1. Give your teacher a list with your GPA, your test scores, and extracurricular activities you are involved in.
2. Include a list of your training in that area and workshops that you have attended.
3. Add theatre camps and special skills.

4. This will help them write a letter about YOU, the person, not just the performer.

Go to your teacher over the summer, or as soon as school starts! Remember that your theatre teachers are as busy as you are. The later you wait, the harder it is to get the letters you need from them. You want them to be able to truly represent you and your potential. **Remember the early bird gets the worm!**

Sample Artistic Letter of Recommendation

To Whom It May Concern:

I wholeheartedly recommend Sample Student for your musical theatre program. I have had the pleasure of working with Sample, both as a private acting coach and a director, for a little over 2 years. During this time, I have seen him develop into a mature and hardworking young man. What excites me the most about Sample is that he has a true passion for the arts as a whole.

Sample is not afraid to admit when he is wrong, or if he is lacking in a certain area. He truly wants to be the best he can be in everything that he does. This young man has devoted the last two years to his theatrical training, spending almost every day at the studio in dance classes, acting technique classes, voice lessons, acting lessons, and show rehearsals. He tackles every challenge that is thrown at him and constantly tries to find the lessons to be learned in each situation.

Beyond performing, Sample has a passion for playwriting and directing as well. He truly values the whole creative process which can make him a dream to work with. He quickly has become an actor that I enjoy working with because of what he brings to the creative process. The one thing that I truly respect about him is that he always has something positive to say about every theatrical experience that he has. His is always the number one cheerleader and supporter both for the project he is involved with, and his fellow castmates. He looks at each show he auditions for as an experience to learn something new, constantly wanting to challenge himself with new and contrasting roles. Over the last two years I have been able to cast him in a variety of roles and every time he exceeds my expectations.

Of course, with every young artist, there are areas that still need growth. If I had to mention one area that Sample needs to grow that would be his ability to accept his accomplishments and not beat himself up about minor changes, he "could have made". Sometimes Sample can be his own worst enemy, which can create setbacks, but he rebounds quickly with a new understanding of where growth is needed. This is an area that we are working on and he is making progress.

I have no doubt that Sample has a future in the arena. His passion for the creation of art, matched with his incredible work ethic, is setting him on an incredible path. I truly think that he will be a positive addition to any musical theatre department. Sample continues to impress me with his knowledge, skills, and dedication to his work. I believe you will find him to be a student whose talents will only shine further through his pursuit of education at your institution. Feel free to contact me if you require further information.

Sincerely,

Teacher Name
Private Acting Coach

FINANCIAL AID AND COLLEGE SCHOLARSHIPS

College Scholarships are very important for students. There are many different types of scholarships available for performers. We will attempt to help you understand this process.

The most important source of scholarships are academic. To get the most academic money available, you need to have the highest GPA and test scores possible.

1. The first thing to know is that academic rigor is less important than a high GPA for most schools. You are better off to take Honors and on-level courses and have a high A than to take AP courses and have a low A or a B.
2. Every student should take the ACT/SAT tests during their Junior year. The higher the test scores, the more academic money is available for you. Make sure that if the scores go up, you send new information to your schools to raise your chances of scholarship.
3. College Honors programs usually come with money from the school, as well as perks like registering early, smaller class sizes and/or special housing or living communities.

After academic money, you need to look at talent-based scholarships.

1. The reality is that full talent-based scholarships are usually held for students from low income homes or difficult circumstances.

2. Each school has a different level of talent scholarships, and usually range from $500-$4000 a year. These are helpful as every little bit counts.

In-state tuition is something that many schools can offer.

1. Because some states do not have a BFA Musical Theatre degree available through their state schools, they have reciprocal agreements with schools in other states that offer in-state tuition rates to out-of-state students who qualify.
2. This significantly lowers your costs, and can make out of state schools affordable. It is your responsibility to ask for as much as you can.
3. Do not be afraid to ask for financial assistance, the schools have money to spend and it is part of their budget.
4. If you have a good scholarship offer from a school, you can let the other schools know what amount they need to match.

Finally, there are hundreds, if not thousands, of small quirky scholarships.

1. Google college scholarships and you will find many categories.
2. Talk to your human resources representative at your work (or your parents' work), church, and community groups. Many of these organizations will offer small scholarships.
3. Remember that every $500 that doesn't come out of your own pocket is a gift!

In the second year, many schools will offer opportunities for students to be the Resident Advisor in their dorms. This usually pays for housing and food and is a huge benefit to students. The leadership qualities they are looking for are the very qualities that most artistic students share. As housing and food are quite expensive, this can be a huge boost for the next 2-3 years.

WORKSHEET B
COLLEGE AUDITION TIMELINE

COMPLETE DURING JUNE/JULY/AUGUST –

Summer following Junior Year and BEFORE SENIOR YEAR!

- By the end of June, finalize your Pre-Screen Audition Package that should include:
    - ➤ 1 contemporary song
    - ➤ 1 pre-1965 songs
    - ➤ 1 Contemporary comedic monologue
    - ➤ 1 Contemporary dramatic monologue
    - ➤ 1 Shakespeare monologue
    - ➤ 1 Pre-1900 heightened language monologue

- MAKE A SPREADSHEET that lists
  (If you are a CAP student you can do this all in your Navigator)
    - ➤ Name of Schools
    - ➤ College Application deadlines
    - ➤ College Entrance Requirements
    - ➤ Musical Theatre/Acting Program Requirements (Song/monologue(s) cuts and/or timing)
    - ➤ Pre-Screen requirements and deadlines
    - ➤ Live audition requirements and deadlines
    - ➤ Dance audition details
    - ➤ Audition dates & locations
    - ➤ If they will be at any Unified Auditions

- FOR AUDITION SONGS: Make all cuts with the help of a qualified, experience musical theatre vocal coach - 16, 32 bar, one minute, 30 seconds, 90 seconds, two minute cuts. CAP professionals are always available for this process!
- FOR AUDITION MONOLOGUES: Make all cuts needed in your monologues - one minute, 90 seconds and two minutes. We suggest using a professional instructor to help you with this as well. CAP professionals are always available for this process!
- Practice, Practice, Practice your cuts for the specific packages of songs/monologues to reflect the pre-screen requirements. Choose the best monologue and contrasting songs for the pre-screen. Time everything several times and meet all requirements.
- Private lessons in dance will be required in order to choreograph what is required for the pre-screen videos.

AUGUST/SEPTEMBER/OCTOBER/NOVEMBER

- Begin working on College applications (to get accepted into the COLLEGE – not the musical theatre program). College essays are written and SAT/ACT tests are taken - again.

- Start and complete your FAFSA application. Most schools can't finalize scholarship offers until parents have applied.

- After the College applications are completed, begin applications to the musical theatre programs.
  College and Program applications are separate. Keep accurate records of all applications.

- If you are planning on attending CAP United Auditions you will need to register and book your travel and hotel. Make travel plans for National Unified auditions in Chicago, New York or Los Angeles if you plan on attending.

- Set up an account with getacceptd.com. This allows you to upload your pre-screen video, headshot, and resume.

- Record Pre-Screen Videos. Check with each school to see when they open pre-screen submission and what the deadlines may be. All material must be practiced and then practiced even more. Pre-Screen videos do not have to be professionally recorded but should be well-prepared with all correct requirements. Good lighting and good sound are A MUST!!!!

- As soon as pre-screens are recorded, begin working on live audition requirements. Some programs have live auditions in October so be ready. Audition season is October – March.

- Complete all college and program applications.

- Order transcripts from your high school to be sent to colleges. This process can take up to 4 – 6 weeks, especially if your school is busy with other student's requests.

- Check the recommendation requirements and start lining up the teachers who will be writing your recommendation letters. Pay close attention to the EXACT recommendations needed: academic, leadership, talent, etc. Plan accordingly so specific recommendation letters are not duplicated or one of the recommendation requirements left out.

DECEMBER/JANUARY/FEBRUARY/MARCH

- Keep working and re-working your college audition material. Some changes may need to be made depending on the school for which you are auditioning.
- Keep healthy, organized and as calm as possible. Planning is crucial for the audition season. The more planning you can do ahead of time, the more enjoyable the audition process will be.
- Take the SAT and ACT one last time for the best score possible
- Double and triple check that all transcripts, test scores, essays, headshots, specific musical theatre program applications, essays, and references have been received by the schools for which you are applying.

APRIL

- Sort out acceptances/wait lists/ deferrals/rejections. If there are any schools that you have not visited and that you are seriously considering, now is the time to visit the campus.

MAY

- College decisions should be made by May 1st. In fact, many schools require a decision by May 1st. It is considered the National reply-by date.

The college audition process can be grueling, exhausting and stressful. Remember the passion you have for musical theatre and try to be as eager as possible to show the world how much you have worked toward your college dream. Every audition is a chance to "perform" and... isn't that what you love to do? For parents, try not to fall into the compulsive trap and become hyper-invested in the college audition process. Parents and family are the stabilizing factor while your child is going through such emotional highs and lows and will need you to remain as objective as possible!

Need Scheduling Help?
Get a consult with a CAP Scheduling Coach!

WORKSHEET C
BUDGET WORKSHEET

* Fill this out for each school to which you are applying

School Name: _____

APPLICATION & AUDITION COST

Application Fee:_____

PreScreen Fee:_____

Audition Fee:_____

Travel Cost: _____

Total:_____

YEARLY SCHOOL COST

Yearly Tuition:_____

Room/Board:_____

Extra Fees:_____

Books/Supplies:_____

Total:_____

School Name:_____

APPLICATION & AUDITION COST

Application Fee:_____

PreScreen Fee:_____

Audition Fee:_____

Travel Cost: _____

Total:_____

YEARLY SCHOOL COST

Yearly Tuition:_____

Room/Board:_____

Extra Fees:_____

Books/Supplies:_____

Total:_____

Chapter Three

KNOWING YOUR TYPE

"What's my type?" is a question that all actors must ask themselves. Knowing the answer to this question informs decisions that you make as student actor and as a professional. Everyone has a type. There is no escaping it and once you know what your type is you can work with that information to help you with casting. However, not knowing your type or working against your type makes getting cast or selected for a school so much harder.

If you're not sure of your type, let's talk about how to get this vital information and apply it to your college audition process. Your type is determined by multiple factors - your sex, your age, your physical characteristics, your voice, and your personality.

Here are a *few* examples of types:

Ingenue: An ingenue is the young innocent of the show. For example: Cosette in Les Miserables, Maria in West Side Story, Sarah Brown in Guys and Dolls. Disney uses this type for a lot of their princesses - Ariel, Belle, Anna in Frozen, etc. Sometimes an ingenue can have a little quirky energy (Rapunzel) or a little more sassy energy (Laurie in Oklahoma) or very spirited energy (Jo in Little Women).

Leading Lady: Leading Ladies are a little more mature than the Ingenue. Iconic Leading Ladies include Delores in Sister Act, Elphaba in Wicked, Reno in Anything Goes, and Dolly Levi in Hello Dolly.

Bad Boy: Bad boys include Stanley in A Street Car Named Desire, Danny in Grease, Ren McCormack in Footloose and Sky Masterson in Guys and Dolls.

Leading Man: Leading man roles range from Gaylord Ravenal in Show Boat to Henry Higgins in My Fair Lady; from Jamie in Last Five Years to Chad in All Shook Up.

Character Actors: Character acting roles are varied and apply to men and women alike. Le Fou in Beauty and the Beast, The Baker in Into The Woods, Ali Hakim in Oklahoma, Mrs. Hannigan in Annie (*basically, any role that Carol Burnett plays*), Hedy LaRue in How to Succeed In Business Without Really Trying, Ado Annie in Oklahoma, etc.

These are just the basic types of actors, but there are variations of these types and many others to consider.

To find your type try a few of these suggestions:

1. Ask your acting coach, other teachers, friends and family what actor you remind them of and look up those actors.

2. Research those performers and the roles they have played. Watch videos of those roles played by various performers. What's their voice type and vocal range?
3. Make a list of characteristics that these roles share. Do these characteristics sound like a part of you in some way? Can you bring these characteristics to life on stage?
4. Look for other roles who share some of those characteristics.

Remember that as you age, your type will change, but knowing your type as you enter college auditions is imperative to choosing quality audition material and showing college faculty that not only are you a smart actor, but a marketable one as well.

Choose material that suits your type. If you are a classic Disney ingenue, you should avoid songs like "Number 5 With A Bullet" from High Fidelity. If you are a quirky male side-kick character actor, you want to sing something like "What Chance Have I With Love" from Louisiana Purchase and avoid material meant for a leading man like "You Are Love" from Showboat. This same concept applies to monologues. Stay within the range of your type!

Your type should also influence the clothes you wear for auditions. The quirky character actress should probably avoid wearing the soft, pastel A-line dress made of lace material. Consider wearing something that you would feel great wearing to a party such as a flattering pair of pants, tailored jacket, trendy accessories or simple necklace and a fantastic pair of shoes or boots. Men may have fewer options in expressing their type in their clothing, but a nice pair of shoes, a fun print or a cool tie can give a hint of who you are and your type.

Keep in mind that some schools are looking for specific types during their audition process. If they have a strong character actress graduating from their program that year, they will probably be looking for a replacement for her during their auditions. However, if they already have four blonde-haired, blue-eyed ingenues, they are probably going to pass on girls of that type no matter how incredibly talented they are.

In other words, your type matters in many college decisions and it would be unwise to take a rejection personally. Many times, college faculty will admire a performer's talent and personality but they simply don't have room in their program for that type that year. Decisions are sometimes based on type, not talent. Instead of being discouraged by a rejection, try to focus on looking for those programs that are looking for your type and will know how to train and prepare you for the professional world.

Need Help Finding Your Type?
Get a consult with a CAP Coach!

WORKSHEET D
FINDING YOUR TYPE

1. What performer/performers do you feel you most embody? Are you more of a Sutton Foster, Jeremy Jordan, Patty Lupone or Alex Brightman? It may feel weird to say that you are like a famous performer, however this can be a good start to finding material that works for you.

2. List the last 5 roles you have played?

3. Do you see any similarities in these roles? List those similarities:

4. Let's say that you are an ingenue, however there is a big difference between Laurie in Oklahoma and Wednesday Addams from Addams Family. List three adjectives to describe the types of characters you relate to the most:

1:_____ 2:_____ 3:_____

5. Not every girl has to wear a dress and not every guy needs to wear a tie. Describe your favorite outfit, something that you might wear for a night out or to a casual event:

6. Ask the people closest to you to describe you in one word. Make a list of those words and see if they help you construct an outline for your type. What are those words

Chapter Four

AUDITION MATERIAL SELECTIONS

MONOLOGUES

Frequently, students of the arts believe that great acting should not take a lot of effort or training because, "You just have to be real, right?" If only it were that easy! The reality is that quality acting that seems real and effortless usually takes a lot of training and guidance.

There are many ways to go about getting this training, but we'll mention a few techniques that actors will want to be familiar with and seek more in-depth training in order to prepare for college level auditions and training. There is also a worksheet at the end of this chapter that can help you get started with your monologue.

In a perfect world, a performer should have roughly five to seven monologues well prepared with one minute, 90 second and 2 minute cuts of each. Many schools will require that your monologues are from published plays. These monologues should NEVER come from a free website or from Film/TV. Your audition repertoire should include two contemporary dramatic monologues, two contemporary comedic monologues, a classical monologue (consult your acting coach because dates of "classical" monologues can be subjective, but most agree that this means material written before 1900), and a Shakespeare monologue (only a handful of musical theater programs ask for a Shakespeare monologue, but you have to be prepared). Of course, a performer can always add to their repertoire with extra material that shows more variety of what they can do.

Be careful that you choose material that shows who YOU are. The monologues need to be age appropriate, avoid extensive profanity, and nothing overly depressing. Choose material that will highlight your ability to connect with "your person" (don't choose material that has you talking about something, but instead that shows a conversation between you and someone else). Show detailed reactions to "your person", and use the opportunity to be vulnerable and find the love in the relationship. Keep in mind that love can take on a lot of different forms and it can be very complicated in human relationships, so we're not saying to just be sweet and cooperative.

Make sure that you don't fall into the trap of crying or yelling through your material. No one wants to sit in a room for several hours and watch performer after performer shout, scream profanity, or cry in hopeless despair. They want to see that you understand human interaction in all of its complexity and beauty. They want to see you struggle and work for what you want from "your person". They want to see an arc to this conversation, a peak in the emotions and struggle, and then a final resolution.

For help in connecting to material in this way, you will need an acting coach who understands basic techniques like Stanislavski, Uta Hagen, Stanford Meisner, and/or Michael Shurtleff. We suggest each performer get a copy of Michael Shurtleff's book "Auditions". A careful study of Shurtleff's "12 Guideposts" will go a long way in helping a young performer bring more authenticity and connection to their material. All these acting principles can be applied to monologues as well as all songs.

Performer's need time with material, both songs and monologues, to fully explore the emotional options of each piece. Memorizing the actual words of the song and monologue is only a basic step in the process of preparing your audition material. Breaking the material down using the well-respected acting principles takes time and guidance from a knowledgeable teacher.

Once the material is chosen, broken down and practiced, copies of each cut can be copied and placed in the back of your audition book for quick reference.

In the audition room, take a moment before you begin to collect yourself and focus your energy. Bring your eyes up, see your person and begin. At the end of each piece, make sure that you hold the energy for a moment. Don't fall out of your storytelling immediately. Give everyone a moment or two to process what has happened and then release.

If you are asked to do any material again, that is a good sign! No one takes time to work with a performer, unless they are interested in you and your work. Usually, when they ask you to do the song or monologue again, they will also give you a "re-direct", meaning that they will ask you to perform the material again but with a slight change or variation. Go with it! Be flexible! It is not important that you understand what they are looking for. They may simply be looking to see if you can adjust on the spot. This is the time to take risks and throw yourself completely into their instructions!

Need Monologue Help?
Get a consult with a CAP Acting Coach!

WORKSHEET E
MONOLOGUE PREP

Who are you talking to?

It is important to decide who you are talking to in your monologue. Let's say that the person in your monologue is talking to their mom who abandoned them when they were young. Unless you have the same type of strained relationship with your own mother it is going to be difficult to use your mom as the person you are talking to during your monologue. However, you can substitute another person in your life that you feel may have abandoned you or wasn't there for you. So, even though your character is talking to their mom, you can be using this other person from your real life as a stand in for this relationship.

The Moment Before:

Every monologue (and song) should have a "moment before" that you can either create from the setting of the play or create from your own experiences. Spend time creating this "moment before" in detail. Write out dialogue if that helps, but at least create a singular line that the person you are talking to says that makes you say the first line of your monologue. This allows you to be in the moment when you start, instead of starting cold.

What do you want?

Deciding what your character wants or needs is the fuel for the entire monologue. We more commonly call this our objective. Make sure that your objective is something that you can't give up on, that you fight until the end to get. If your objective is weak there is no reason for your character to keep jumping over the obstacles. Try to keep it to a one sentence answer. If you have to explain it in too many words odds are you haven't quite searched deep enough to find the center. Try to keep the objective focused on something you can relate to, something you could see yourself fighting for.

Where are you?

Defining the environment of your monologue is just as important as who you are talking to during it. Make sure that the environment is some place that is familiar to you. No need to re-create the wheel. Also, make sure that you pick an environment that works for you, not against you. If you need to be vulnerable with the person you are talking to, don't set the monologue in a busy restaurant. Also, try to create a space that you can be active, sitting in a car might be comfortable but it doesn't allow you to incorporate your body!

Now fill this out for each of your monologues:

Who am I talking to?

_____

What is my relationship to that person?

_____
_____

Where are we?

_____
_____

What do I want?

_____
_____

What just happened?

_____
_____
_____
_____

SONGS

There are specific vocal skills that each student should demonstrate during prescreens and live auditions.

Most auditions (*there are exceptions to this rule, so read each school's requirements carefully*) will require two contrasting songs: one from the contemporary time period (post-1965) and one from the classic musical theater time period (pre-1965). The songs should also contrast in voice co-ordinations (*one song should demonstrate "mix"/legit coordination and the other song should demonstrate "mix"/belt coordination*), tempo, style, etc. The one characteristic that both songs should share is that both fit the type of the singer you are.

For example, a larger woman with strong facial features and a character sounding voice should not sing songs that are traditionally sung by ingenues (*the young innocent, frequently with romantic interest*). It would be equally confusing for a man who looks and behaves like a traditional leading man (*i.e. Hugh Jackman, Gene Kelly, Jeremy Jordan, etc*) to sing songs that are meant for the quirky, awkward side-kick character. Songs should match the singer's type and vocal tone.

Balance and control through the first passagio (E4-F#4 for men and A4-C#5 for women) should be demonstrated in both songs. If you have easy and impressive control of your second passagio (A4-C#5 for men and E5-F#5 for women), then certainly choose material that will highlight those skills. However, DO NOT choose material that is beyond your vocal ability or material that exposes what you struggle with. As stated before, do NOT show what you are bad at.

Each song will need to have a 32 bar and a 16 bar cut made for auditions. These cuts should include the most challenging sections of the song. We suggest this for two reasons: first, the challenging section of a song usually contains the emotional climax as well, and including this within your cut will give your acting arc and intensity. Secondly, if the challenging section is left out of the cut the adjudicators may wonder why it was not included and ask to hear you tackle that section at some point during the vocal audition. So, when choosing, stick to songs in which you are certain you are able master the most challenging part.

For each cut, find a pianist who can create tracks that match the cuts exactly. You will not use tracks at on campus live auditions, but you will need them for prescreens (*unless you want to add the expense of a pianist while you record*) and for many auditions at National Unifieds. These tracks should be loaded onto your phone and on a back-up location (*i.e. Dropbox, iPad, extra phone, etc*) and organized in a way that they are easily accessible.

For college musical theater auditions, do NOT change the key of the piece. Sometimes songs are not published in the same key that the song was recorded in, so be attentive to the key when acquiring sheet music. Use cast albums as the guide, in general. If the songs were recorded in a specific key, make sure that the published sheet music is in that same key or have it transposed to the recorded key if needed. This "rule" may be overlooked with older material that has been recorded in various keys over the decades and it doesn't apply to pop/rock songs, especially when used as a "gender-bender" song.

In addition to having 32 bar cuts and 16 bar cuts inside your audition books, you should include copies of the full songs of all your cuts in case you are asked to sing a different part of the song (*if your cuts include the most challenging sections, this is rarely a request by auditors but it is better to be over prepared*). Audition books should also include eight other musical theater songs of various decades, composers, tempos, emotional content, and styles that, of course, fit your tone and type. Along with the ten musical theater songs (*including one or two songs from roles that you have been cast in and have mentioned on your resume*), include at least one pop/rock song. All songs that are placed in the audition book should be mastered and completely memorized. If you struggle in anyway with material, it should never be placed in the audition book.

You must understand the style of each song. For songs that demonstrate "legit" coordination, you should demonstrate long legato lines, sustained notes with vibrato and rounded vowels with a lifted soft palate. For belt songs, you should show a great sense of the rhythm of the piece with shorter phrasing, wider vowels, less vibrato, etc. The styles of each piece should be thoroughly researched, studied and applied in your own unique way. Singing a belt song with long, smooth phrases and covered vowels shows a lack of understanding for the material. Likewise, singing a Golden Age legit song with short phrasing, no vibrato and forward placed vowels is a mockery of material. Consider the style carefully.

Choose a voice instructor that can help you navigate the many requirements and challenges of tutoring the vocal instrument, choosing appropriate material, teaching the style of each piece and helping you stay in top vocal shape.

The best vocal instructor can help you, but only you can take care of your instrument and keep it healthy. This is referred to as vocal hygiene and its importance cannot be overstated.

Here are some key points to good vocal hygiene:

1. Hydrate! Your vocal folds are covered in a moist layer of skin-like covering called the epithelium. However, if you don't drink water consistently, the covering becomes dry and less effective in buffering the impact of the vocal folds as you speak and sing. The goal is to take in roughly 8 ounces of water each hour throughout the day. You should drink enough water that you have to use the restroom multiple times a day and that each time you relieve yourself, your urine is pale yellow or clear. Drinking huge amounts of water at one time will not keep you hydrated as your body can

only absorb so much water at a time. Small and consistent intake of water throughout your day is key.

2. Sleep! Your body cannot recuperate if you don't sleep for long stretches of time, and this includes the muscles and tissues of the vocal folds and larynx. Your goal should be for 7 - 8 hours of uninterrupted sleep each night.

3. Vocal exercises! Singers should move their voices through their range using a variety of co-ordinations, scales and exercises. Singing songs does not count as exercises. Keeping those tissues responsive and warm is essential to staying in peak condition and continuously improving your vocal technique.

4. Wash your hands! If you get sick, your voice will be affected, sometimes drastically. This could lead to a significant disappointment if your voice isn't functioning well on the day of an important audition. The first defense to avoiding illness is washing your hands well multiple times a day: after bathroom use, after touching door handles, pianos, anything that has a lot of human contact. Try to keep your fingers away from your eyes, nose and mouth.

5. Take vitamins and eat a healthy diet! Get blood tests done to see which vitamins your body is low on and consult a doctor on how to improve your vitamin and mineral balance. Stay away from high-sugar, low-nutrient foods that undermine your immune

system. Include healthy vegetables, proteins, fats and carbohydrates into your diet.

6. Get acid reflux treated ASAP! Many singers struggle with acid reflux and either ignore the symptoms or don't even realize they are experiencing them. A trip to a good Ear Nose and Throat doctor (ENT) should tell you the health of your voice and if acid reflux is a concern. If it is, address it immediately! It will tax your voice drastically.

7. When struggling with an illness or an over-taxed voice, use Semi Occluded Vocal Tract (SOVT) exercises and Resonant Voice Exercises. SOVT exercises include straw exercises, puffy cheek exercises, lip trill/buzzing exercises on various scales (visit the website www.CemMusicStudio.com to see demonstration videos of these exercises). Resonant Voice Exercises include sounds such as "mmm", "zzz", "vvv" on various scales (visit the website www.CemMusicStudio.com to see demonstration videos of these exercises). Ginger is a known anti-inflammatory and can help reduce swelling in tissues. Use it as a spice in food, eat it raw or pour hot water over ginger slices and steep for tea. Throat Coat Tea and other teas are helpful in soothing tissues, but keep in mind that anything you ingest never directly touches your vocal folds. Food and drink travels down your esophagus, not your windpipe, so the benefits from ginger products or any tea or honey may take a couple of days to be noticeable since your body needs time to digest the food and absorb the nutrients.

8. Humidifiers can be helpful for hydration when air conditioners, central heating, airline travel or dry hotel rooms leave you feeling dry. Nebulizers filled with purified salt water can also help with hydration. Keep all equipment clean and free from dirt or mold.

9. For allergy sufferers, consider using a Neti Pot or another sinus rinse throughout the day, but especially before sleeping to clear out allergens in the sinus cavities, thereby reducing inflammation. Make sure that you use purified water at all times! Serious health issues arise from using tap water. Also, make sure that all the water has drained from the sinuses before going to sleep.

10. Exercise! Get your blood moving throughout the tissues of your body through varied daily exercise. Not only does this help you maintain a healthy weight, but exercise supports a healthy immune system which means less illness for you. Doing a few minutes of exercise before vocal warm ups encourages blood flow and prepares tissues in the larynx for use.

Need Vocal Help?
Get a consult with a CAP Vocal Coach!

WORKSHEET F

CHECKLIST FOR YOUR MUSICAL AND VOCAL NEEDS

Make sure you have completed the following steps or acquired these items for the music portion of your audition:

- Your completed audition book should travel with you as a carry on, never put it in your checked luggage.
- Make a digital copy of your song cuts and upload them to a service (Google Docs, Dropbox, etc.) that you can access anywhere.
- Download all your song tracks to an easy to access file on your cell phone. Make sure the songs are downloaded so you do not require internet access to play them. You may be in places where the WIFI or internet connection is poor.
- Song tracks should only be a piano track (no orchestration) and should be cut to match your cut of the song exactly.
- Some schools ask for a repertoire list, so have a couple copies of the repertoire you've worked on over the last two to three years and place them in the back of your audition book in case you are asked for a list.
- Organize your audition book in a way that makes it easy for you to find your songs very quickly. Add a Table of Contents page to the front of your audition book so college faculty can scan your contents quickly.

Audition season is prime time for illness to set in because of the travel and stress, so make sure you have the following items on hand to help protect your voice through your auditions:

- Vogmask or medical mask to wear on airplanes or any public transport
- Hand sanitizer
- Nebulizer for hydrating vocal folds with purified salt water
- Steamer for loosening compacted mucous in the sinuses
- Herbal Tea with lemon and ginger
- Sip straws for straw exercises (see the video on YouTube of Dr. Ingo Titze demonstrating straw exercises) for vocal balance and health

- Lemon and peppermint essential oils to relieve sore throat discomfort. Apply lemon oil first to the outside of the neck where the pain is concentrated, and then apply peppermint oil over the lemon oil.
- Recording of full vocal warm ups for you to use before auditions and a recording of "sick" vocal warm ups for you to use in case you are ill and need a modified warm up routine.
- Acetaminophen based medicine for pain control. Avoid any pain control medication that uses NSAIDs (Non-steroidal Anti-inflammatory Drugs) as these types of medications can make singers more prone to injury when combined with illness and intense vocal demands.

WORKSHEET G

CHOOSING SONGS FOR YOUR AUDITION BOOK

1. Choose songs that fit your type. See the song section of the book if you need a more in depth description of "type". Remember that high school and community theatre casting is not necessarily an accurate reflection of your type since they have a smaller pool of performers to choose from, so frequently you may have been cast in roles that professionally you would not be considered for because it doesn't fit your type. Colleges will always look at you from a professional perspective, since that is the world for which you are paying them to prepare you to enter.
2. Choose songs that show off your unique vocal qualities and do NOT emphasize what you are still working on vocally. Always show them what you're good at, never what you struggle with!
3. Choose songs that are not terribly over-done.
4. Choose song cuts that have an arc and show some vocal and acting chops.

10 Roles You Could Be Cast In Today...

1_____

2_____

3_____

4_____

5_____

6_____

7_____

8_____

9_____

10_____

What Songs Fit These Roles...

_____

_____

_____

_____

_____

_____

_____

_____

_____

_____

_____

_____

_____

_____

_____

Tips for Discovering New Songs

- Look up musical theatre composers and note every show they've worked on. Are there shows on that list that you haven't heard of? Go listen to the cast recording of these newly discovered shows or look up YouTube videos of other performers singing these songs.
- Look up an actor/actress that shares your type. Research their career and the works they've been a part of. You may discover that they've worked on shows of which you were not aware. Look at other actors/actresses who played the same roles and look up their careers.

- Search "Tony Award Nominees for Best Score 1968", or 1977 or 1989. Look at the nominees for Best Score. You will discover shows that you have never heard of, but obviously there's some great music in that score because they were nominated for a Tony Award.

Narrowing Down Your Song Options

Make sure that as you make the final choices about which songs to include in your audition book, you have songs that cover these categories. Check each category off as you find the song that meets the requirement.

- Up-tempo song
- Ballad song
- Contemporary song (written after 1970)
- Golden Age song (written before 1965)
- Song that shows "mix" voice and "belt" voice
- Song that shows "classical" voice (long phrasing, resonant "head" voice, control of vibrato)
- Song with emotional drive
- Song from a role you've listed on your resume
- Pop/Rock song
- Song you can sing really well even when you're sick

Keep in mind that you can have songs that check off a few of the above categories. You are looking to have between six to eight musical theatre songs and two or three pop/rock songs in your audition book, so in the end you will end up with eight to ten songs in your book.

Make a 32 bar and 16 bar cut of each musical theatre song. The pop/rock songs can each be cut to between roughly sixty to ninety seconds.

It is always best to get an unbiased opinion on your song selections, so make sure you talk over your options with a trusted voice teacher, director or college audition coach. As always, the CAP team is here to help you, so reach out to us if you need any guidance.

AUDITION BOOK

ASSEMBLING YOUR AUDITION BOOK

One important component of a solid audition is having a well-organized and professional looking audition book. Below are steps to help you create the perfect audition book that you will use for years to come.

1. Gather all the 16 bar and 32 bar cuts of your songs. Also have a copy of the full song for each cut. You can also place copies of all your Monologues in your audition book.

2. Copy the cuts onto white card stock. The card stock makes page turns much easier for your pianist. Mark each cut and full song with a highlighter drawing attention to anything that you will need to discuss with your audition pianist - tempo changes, fermatas, key changes, etc.

3. Have a three-hole punch ready.

4. Purchase heavy duty, NON-GLARE sheet protectors. These sheet protectors are significantly heavier in weight than a regular sheet protector and have a matte finish so there is no glare off the surface.

5. Purchase a 1.5-2 inch heavy duty binder with a plastic sleeve on the front (for you to place one of your headshots in so your Book is easily identifiable). There are also inexpensive, black leather

binders that fit this description and are very professional looking. Make sure that the binder can easily open flat.

6. Purchase heavy duty dividers. You will need one for each of the following sections: 16 bar, 32 bar, Full Song, Pop, Monologues, and Headshot/Resume.

7. Go over with your voice teacher or a pianist what would be the easiest page turns for an audition pianist if your cut is 3 pages long. After they've shown you the easiest page turn, three-hole punch the cut (printed on white card stock) so that it accommodates the audition pianist with the easiest page turn. Tape the pages that are back to back together on the top, bottom and sides so they are secure. Slip the three-hole punched and taped cut into the heavy duty, non-glare sheet protectors. Every cut that is only 2 pages should be three-hole punched so that the pages face each other. This eliminates a page turn for the pianist. Your job is to make their life easy, so they can play your pieces to their best ability. Once each cut is three-hole punched and taped correctly, place it in the sheet protectors so that the same page turns are in place (the three holes from the punch should be on the same side of holes on the sheet protector).

8. Place full songs in the sheet proctors as well. You don't need to worry about page turns with full songs.

9. Place an extra headshot/resume (we suggest that you always carry 10 extra) in its own sheet protector. This protects the

headshots from getting scratched by the staples that are on other headshot/resumes in your binder.

10. Alphabetize your 16 bar cuts and place them all behind a divider labeled "16 Bars". Alphabetize your 32 bar cuts and place them behind a divider labeled "32 Bars". Alphabetize your full songs and place them behind the divider labeled "Full Songs". Alphabetize your pop songs and place them behind a divider labeled "Pop Songs". Alphabetize you monologues and place them behind a divider labeled "Monologues"

11. Place all your headshots and resumes at the very back under a divider labeled "Headshot/Resume".

12. Create a table of contents of every cut and song within your book and place the Table of Contents at the very front of your book for easy reference.

13. If an audition pianist doesn't like sheet protectors (although most pianists are good with the heavy duty, non-glare kind), you can easily accommodate them by pulling your music out of the sheet protectors and placing the music straight into the binder, because you have already three-hole punched it. This method takes all preferences into consideration.

WORKING WITH A PIANIST

If you're not accustomed to working with a live pianist, it would may be worth it to book some time with a local pianist who can go over your music with you and help you practice the following steps:

1. Greet your pianist with a smile, introduce yourself and thank them for playing for you.

2. Set your audition book on their music stand and open it to your first song.

3. Point out anything in the song that you want to draw their attention to, such as: fermatas, crescendos, repeats, key changes, time signature change, etc.

4. Give the pianist your tempo for the song by singing a few bars of the song. Don't snap your fingers or clap your hands for the tempo. Some pianists find that condescending – just sing a few bars.

5. Repeat steps 3 and 4 for your second song.

6. If you have a monologue in between your two songs, explain that to the pianist.

7. Tell the pianist that you'll give them a nod when you are ready to begin.

8. If something goes wrong with the music you NEVER blame the pianist. Make the best of it and move on with the audition.

9. After the college faculty have completed your audition, make sure you pick up your music from the pianist and thank them again for playing for you.

WARDROBE

Part of getting your college audition package ready is your wardrobe. First, dress for your type. Dressing for your type shows others that you understand who you are and how you are perceived. It doesn't mean you can't add an item that is outside of your type or a little unusual, especially if it holds sentimental value or has a special meaning for you. You don't have to dress up in a suit and tie. You could pair a great blazer with a nice pair of jeans and fantastic pair of stylish shoes that show a little of your personality. We knew one young man who was auditioning for colleges and he was clearly a quirky, side-kick, character actor type. He decided to go with the traditional slacks and button down shirt, but then took the opportunity to show his personality with a Batman bow tie. It was perfect for him! And, perfectly his type! Plus, a great conversation piece! By the time he left the audition room, college faculty felt like they really knew who he was. That was an unusual and perfect addition to his outfit and smart marketing strategy.

Make sure that your clothing is flattering to your figure. You don't have to be a size 2, women, but you do need to know how to package the figure you have.

A few suggestions will help you to get closer to finding a great audition wardrobe.

First, listen to a professional stylist! Get someone's opinion who knows and understands fashion and the way it can be used to present you in your best light. It's not always easy to look in the mirror and see yourself and your clothing objectively, so get someone's opinion who is unbiased and knowledgeable.

Secondly, if the fit of the clothing isn't great right off the rack, buy a size larger than required and have the clothing altered to your measurements by a tailor. This takes a little more time and planning, but it doesn't cost much and, quite frankly, well-tailored clothes make an enormous difference in how they complement you. Inexpensive clothing that has been well-tailored can make you look like a million bucks! Give yourself enough time to figure out what you feel confident and comfortable in. Finding the perfect audition outfit in one day is not realistic and incredibly stressful. Use your time in high school to explore options that fit all the criteria above and help you feel your very best, because CONFIDENCE is your best marketing tool. If you build a wardrobe of options throughout high school, when auditions come around you will have several great choices for outfits.

There's a fine line that needs to be walked for college auditions. You want to show your figure to its very best advantage, but you do not want to show a lot of skin. Keep in mind that most of the people you are auditioning for are not comfortable looking at your considerable cleavage or having intimate knowledge of your undergarments. Dressing for your type and figure will build your confidence in the audition as well as help college faculty know that you are a committed, marketable artist.

HEADSHOT

For an actor, the headshot is one of the most important things they have with them. Sometimes, it is the first thing that potential casting agents, schools or producers may see. Do not ask your best friend/mom/cousin to take some pictures of you in your backyard, unless they are a professional photographer who understands headshot requirements. The headshot needs to be well lit with no shadows on your face, and cropped to your shoulders and up. Wear a flattering color and a shirt with an interesting neckline, but anything below the shoulders isn't going to be seen so it's unimportant. That being said, make sure that you pay attention to your neckline, wearing a shirt that is off the shoulder may leave you looking a little "undressed". Trends in headshots are always changing so don't get too caught up in what's new or cool in headshots, because in six months there will be a completely different trend. Pay attention to the look in your eyes (your eyes should look alive and sparkling) and your smile, or lack thereof. The background should not be distracting. Your hair should be well groomed. Do not allow a lot of editing. Snuffing out a blemish that appeared the day of the shoot is fine, but do not allow your photographer to do any narrowing of the face or other major editing of that type. The headshot must look like you! Allow space in the margin for your name.

Need help with headshots?
Contact CAP today!

WORKSHEET H

HEADSHOTS EXAMPLES

Insert Name

Insert Name

Insert Name

Insert Name

Headshots by Marcigliano Photography

RESUME

Your resume is very important in the college process. It is often the first time the audition panel will be introduced to you, and they will refer back to these many times during the audition process. It is imperative that your resume is professional, simple, and HONEST!

Do not put information on your resume that isn't 100% true. Expect that if you put someone's name on your resume as a teacher or coach, the school will check with that person to see what they think of you.

Important facts to remember:

1. Your resume will help solidify who you are.

2. You do not need to list every show you have ever been in.

3. Too much information is simply too much information.

4. You need a variety of shows and roles on the resume.

5. If you have done any professional work, make sure this is at the top of the list.

6. Give them a variety of shows and roles so they see you can be versatile.

7. List important workshops you've attended, and your training.

8. DO NOT put down that you have taken 15-16 years of dance, unless you are ready to be a professional dancer. It is better to say 2-3 years and then blow them away in the dance portion of the audition.

9. They will know within the first few minutes of the audition if you have stretched the truth. Remember this is their business, their world, their expertise. You cannot fool them.

10. Lastly, DO NOT put something on your resume that is not 100% true. If you say you speak German, be ready to translate something into German.

Try to show them who you are, and why you would grow in their program. Remember that they are looking for someone who they can mold, and who is a hard worker. Do not give them a reason to choose someone else. Be the student that every program wants to work with!

If you have a website, make sure that it is updated and relevant to who you are as a performer. Have a beautiful landing page, a page for your headshots and resume, a page for videos of your best performances and a link to contact you. Also, make sure that all your social media is cleansed of offensive material or photos and videos that don't show you in your best light. Make sure that your posts and comments are such that a college faculty would appreciate them, because students from the programs that are considering you frequently stalk social media. Clean it up!

Need help with you resume?
Get a consult with a CAP Coach!

WORKSHEET I
SAMPLE RESUME

There are many ways you can put together a resume.
Here is just one example on a clean layout for a theatrical resume.

SAMPLE NAME

Actor/Singer

Headshot Thumbnail

Address: 0000 This Way Drive
New York, NY 00000
Phone: 000-000-0000
Email: samplename00@gmail.com

Age: 18
Height 5'7
Hair/Eye Color: Brown/Brown
Vocal Range: Tenor G2 to G5

THEATRE

Show	Role	Company, Director
Pippin	Pippin	Company, Director
Show	Role	Company, Director
Show	Role	Company, Director
Show	Role	Company, Director
Show	Role	Company, Director

TRAINING

Ballet	Cindy Dancer	Dance Til you Drop, 2 years
Skill	Instructor	Company, Dates
Skill	Instructor	Company, Dates
Skill	Instructor	Company, Dates

SPECIAL SKILLS

(List here any skills such as acrobatics, foreign languages, sports, or any other skills that might be unique. Make sure that you could perform these skills on the drop of a dime!)

Chapter Five

PRESCREENS

Prescreens are videos you create of you singing, acting and, in some cases, dancing, which you will submit to the college programs which require them. They use these videos to determine whether they are interested in seeing you in person, either at a Unified or an on-campus audition.

Not every school requires you to submit a prescreen, but each year more schools use these videos to help them streamline their audition process.

Make sure that you do your research regarding the requirements for each school's prescreen submissions. Some schools require two contrasting 32 bar songs and a monologue. Some schools want two contemporary 16 bar songs and two monologues. Every school wants a different kind of slate and you'll need to film each slate separately. (*A slate is a short introduction of yourself and your material. For example: "Hi, I'm Sally Johnson and I will be singing Vanilla Ice Cream from She Loves Me")*

Read the prescreen requirements carefully, as well as the instructions for submitting the videos! Some schools will ask you to upload the videos to a site like www.getacceptd.com and some schools will ask you to load your prescreens onto YouTube (*be sure that you make it a private video*) and send them a link. Some schools that you are auditioning for might be a part of the

Common Prescreen. Much like the Common App, the Common Prescreen has a set of requirements that schools can follow that unifies the process for participating schools. It is still very important to read the requirements for each school thoroughly and make sure that you understand them.

As if all of this wasn't confusing enough, schools change their material and submission requirements from year to year, so if a friend tells you what a college required last year, you'll still need to double check that information for the current year because it has quite possibly changed. If you are a CAP student, go to your Navigator and click on your schools, you will find links to their requirements there!

BEFORE YOU FILM

1. Write out the slate for each school you are submitting to, and have those slates on hand for filming to remind you of the requirements.
2. Have the tracks for your song cuts loaded on your phone or book a live accompanist.
3. Have your acting well practiced for both your songs and monologues.
4. Make sure your voice is completely prepared to perform your songs to the best of your ability.
5. Make sure that you are ready to film dance videos by having practiced the choreography until you feel confident in its execution.

6. Have an audition outfit ready for filming. Remember that many schools will want a full body shot, so outfit yourself head-to-toe!
7. Makeup should be flattering and not too heavily applied. We need to see your eyes and lips, so add a little color. But keep it as natural as possible, while still showing up on film.
8. Set a date to film that is AT LEAST a week before your first deadline! You will run into obstacles in this process. It is very stressful when the deadline is hours away and you are having issues with editing or the submission website is glitchy. Give yourself the gift of time: time to edit, time to upload, time to re-film if necessary, and time to solve problems.

FILMING

So, you have all your material selected and well-rehearsed. Now, it is time to record your pre-screens. Read through and follow the steps below.

GET ORGANIZED

Depending on your list of schools you could end up with as little as 3 or as many as 10 schools that need pre-screens. The difficult part is each school will most likely require varied materials for their pre-screens. So, you will need to make a detailed list of each school and their requirements. Make sure that you include not only the material needed but, also, what type of intro or slate is required. Some schools will also ask for a personal statement that needs to be recorded. You want to make sure that when the recording session is done, you haven't forgotten anything.

COMMON PRESCREEN

Started for the 2019-2020 audition season, the Common Prescreen was organized by Papermill Playhouse in conjunction with numerous musical theatre programs around the nation. The Common Prescreen has a goal of streamlining the prescreen process by designating certain criteria for prescreen entries. They also have established the common verbiage used by these programs to let students know what they need to prepare and how to film these selections.

Things to Know:

1- The Common Prescreen is NOT associated at all with the Common App.

2- There is not a "common" portal to which you will upload all of your videos. You will still submit all videos via whatever the program you are auditioning for is using. For example, if the school says "submit via GetAccepted" you will use that portal to upload your videos.

3- Some programs may be on the list of schools participating in the Common Prescreen but may not actually require prescreens. These programs are recognized with an * by their name. These programs will use the Common Prescreen requirements for any videos that may be needed. For example, if the school has an optional prescreen.

4- It is still necessary for you to check each program's individual prescreen page to see exactly what they are requiring for that audition year.

The Common Prescreen is an exciting new development for the prescreen process and we look forward to seeing the way this may grow and help students better understand what is required of them during prescreens. If you have any questions please reach out to the CAP Team!

CHOOSING YOUR RECORDING DEVICE

Your material will need to be uploaded digitally so the first thing you need to make sure is that the device you use to record has the abilities for the files to be uploaded. It is common for people to use a personal device like an iPad or Smartphone to record prescreens. The camera quality of these devices is often better than the family video camera that most people have. The main objective is that you want to have the best quality possible.

Beyond the actual device, you will want to have some sort of tripod or device stabilizer to use while filming. You don't want to have a shaky video because someone is holding the camera the entire time! Make sure that batteries are fully charged and ready to go, bring any necessary charging cords with you just in case the battery starts to get low. Another thing to check is the available storage capacity of your device. You don't want to have the perfect take only to find out your device didn't record it entirely because storage was low. The use of the Cloud, Dropbox or other file storage programs can aide in this process.

WHAT TO WEAR

By this time, you and your coaches will have decided your type and most likely you have already taken your headshots. You want to wear something in your pre-screens that sells your type and brand. Be aware of the wall color in the place that you are filming, you don't want to blend into it! Because you may need to do shots that are full body it is important that you are dressed to impress from head to toe. Girls, make sure that you wear the appropriate amount of makeup. Even if you are more of a natural look person, you will need to wear makeup. The camera and lighting will wash you out, and you want to look polished and fresh. Your whole look should be as close as possible to what you would look like at an actual in-person audition.

Still need help defining your type?

The CAP team can help, just contact us for a consult!

FRAMING THE SHOT

You will need to check each school individually for the type of shot they want. Some schools will want a close-up shot, waist and above (or closer), while others might want a full body shot. There are schools that will tell you exactly what material selection they want and the accompanying style of framing they want. If a school does not specify then it is a good thing to do at least one-piece full body, and maybe your intro/slate and the other pieces in a closer frame. These videos should NOT be professionally recorded. Don't worry about studio lighting and fancy backdrops. You do NOT need to hire professional videographers or book a studio to record. That being said, you also don't want to record these in your bathroom on selfie mode. Make sure that the background is neutral and your lighting is good! A nice amateur video of you is what they are expecting, remember they are interested in you and your talent, not the quality of your recording equipment.

FILMING MONOLOGUES AND SONGS

Ok, you are ready to start filming your material! The thing that you need to remember is that you want to perform to the device that you are using. Don't put the person you are talking to in your monologue or song to the side of you or out of frame; keep them right there where the device is located, right at the camera! You don't want to *stare* at the camera but you do want to throw your energy and performance towards the area of the filming device. You want the people that watch the video to feel as connected as possible to your material. If your private acting and vocal teachers can be present for your pre-screen recording day, it can help to have them coaching you from the sidelines. If they cannot be there the day of filming, make sure that you take a lesson or two beforehand to have them coach you and do mock recordings, so you are ready for the actual day. You will want to record each selection about 4-6 times to get the quality you need. We suggest filming everything at one time in one selection, and that you give yourself at least 90 minutes or more to get everything filmed without feeling rushed. We suggest starting with your songs, that way your voice is ready to go and not tired after doing your monologues. Get your material recorded first and then worry about your slates and extra pieces!

FILMING DANCE

Your dance pre-screens will be filmed separately from your monologues and songs. A larger space will be needed to record these videos. It can be beneficial to have your dance instructor there to help guide you while filming. These videos will obviously be wide screen and show the entire dance space. Most schools will ask for a musical theatre/jazz combination, showing your best technique and ability. There are some schools that might ask for certain dance techniques to be demonstrated, just like with your songs and monologues, make sure you write everything down beforehand. There are some schools that will also allow you to submit additional videos of different dance styles that you may have additional training in (*for example Tap*), however, only submit these other styles IF you are sufficiently trained in these areas. If you tapped in one show last year, that is not sufficient dance training in tap and those videos might actually hurt you more than help!

PRE-SCREEN VIDEO SELECTIONS

Once you have recorded all your selections, it is important to get recommendations for your private instructors, teachers and/or audition team on what clips to edit and submit. Do not submit anything without getting opinions from others! These prescreen submissions are very important, remember that if you do not pass the prescreen, you can't audition for that school in person. Also, remember that these faculty members are watching hundreds of videos, you need to make sure that your prescreen submission not only meets the requirements but also gets their attention, in a good way!

EDITING YOUR PRE-SCREENS

You now have successfully recorded all your pre-screens and you need to get them ready for each individual school. Programs like iMovie and other free programs you can find online can help edit your clips to create the perfect pre-screen pieces. Remember that these do not need to be professional or creative. Don't add in any special transitions or creative touches digitally, just the material!

Now you are ready to start submitting those pre-screens!

Need Prescreen Help?
Get a consult with a CAP Coach!

WORKSHEET J
PRESCREEN WORKSHEET

* Fill this information out for each school that requires prescreens

School Name:
_____

Slate Requirements:
_____

Song Requirements:
_____

Monologue Requirements:
_____

Dance Requirements:
_____

Any Extra Clips/Videos:
_____

Framing Requirements:
_____

What platform is used for submitting the videos?
_____

Submission Deadline:
_____

Other Important Info:
_____

_____

Chapter Six

LIVE AUDITIONS & CALLBACKS

AUDITION ETIQUETTE

Just a few Do's and Don'ts of college auditions….

1. Your audition begins when you step out of your car or leave your room, so be on your most courteous and professional behavior. People that you meet on the subway, in the elevator or in the hallway may be influential in audition decisions… It's also just a smart way to live.

2. Make sure that you bring a bottle of water and a few healthy snacks in your bag for those long on-campus auditions or for those back-to-back auditions at CAP United or National Unifieds.

3. When waiting outside for your audition, be careful to speak positively and not be involved in any negative conversations, disagreements with a parent or gossip with other students. Not only does it look unprofessional to those who run the auditions, but you need to get centered and have your mind prepared to do your best work in the audition room.

4. Have extra headshots and resumes in your audition book.

5. Smile when you enter the room and say, "Hello!"

6. Stand on the "X" or in the center of the room and wait for the panel to direct you. Some faculty may ask you what material you will use and have a few questions for you or they may direct you right over to the pianist. (Read "Working with a Pianist" for more guidance about talking with your pianist.) It is their room, so take your cues off of them.

7. Once you've spoken to your pianist, stand in the center of the room and when the faculty gives you their attention, slate your name and material *(if you haven't already discussed it with them)*. After your slate, take a short moment to get centered mentally, then give your pianist a nod to let them know you are ready.

8. If something goes wrong with the music, you have two options:

   1. Keep going. Sing as if the pianist isn't there and let them find you. This option means you have to know your music so well that you could sing acapella.
   2. Stop and ask if you can start again. If you stop, find a way to laugh it off or make a quick joke of it. Don't make it too serious or heavy.

9. If something goes wrong with your monologue, you have the same two options:

   1. Keep going and do your best to recover.

2. Stop and ask if you can start again. Same advice applies, find a way to make it light-hearted. Re-center yourself and start again.

10. Sometimes, if they are not pushed for time and they are interested in your work, faculty may ask for a "re-direct". That means they may ask you to do the monologue again, but with a different perspective or a different energy. It doesn't mean they didn't like your work. On the contrary! It means they are interested in you and want to see if you can take direction, so go with it!

11. If the faculty asks some interview questions, always be honest. They want to get to know you. If the honest answer paints you in a negative light, have a way to put a positive spin on it in the end. Something like, "I have struggled with managing stress in the past, but I'm working on some strategies to help me cope with stress and I feel like I'm making good progress!"

12. Keep in mind that college faculty are not looking for perfection. They are looking for human artists who share a similar energy, commitment and perspective with the rest of their department. Mistakes will happen and that's ok! Dealing with your mistakes in a professional way makes a great impression.

13. Make sure that you thank the faculty for their time and also thank the students helping to run the auditions. It's the professional standard.

NATIONAL UNIFIED AUDITIONS

National Unified Auditions generally occur the last week of January through the second weekend in February and are located in New York, Chicago, and Los Angeles. Unifieds is a loosely organized consortium of schools that work together to schedule dates and locations across the country. They come together so that students can audition for several schools in one setting.

Here are a few insider tips about National Unifieds:

1. There is not a way for an individual to contact this organization. Dates and locations are posted online each year at www.unifiedauditions.com.
2. Students MUST schedule their auditions with each individual school. This is part of what we call the "Audition Puzzle". This is explained in more detail in the Timeline Section of this material.
3. Chicago, New York, Los Angeles? Which should I attend? The first thing you want to determine is which city has the most schools for which you want to audition. Not all schools attend each location. Generally speaking, Chicago has the

most number of schools. Make sure you do your homework well in advance before determining which Unifieds you will attend.

4. Make your hotel reservations early. The hotels will fill up quickly.

5. Plan on attending several days of the auditions. Don't try to get it all done in just one day. This is the best use of your travel money, so make it count.

6. Make sure when scheduling your auditions you try to schedule at least one hour between each appointment. It is not unusual for schools to run late with their auditions. In addition there will be several schools that will call you back for a dance audition or will schedule a dance audition at the last minute. By leaving gaps in your schedule you will be prepared for these last minute changes.

7. On the first morning you will want to go down to the main lobby and pick up a list of schools that are in attendance. Once you get this list you will want to walk through the hotel and get a good idea of where each of your schools is located. Some schools may be located at other hotels or facilities, so dress for the weather!

8. We highly suggest leaving time in your schedule for adding some walk-up auditions. This is a great way to expand your selection of colleges without adding additional time and money up front.

9. We suggest all students that go to Unifieds bring one of their parents with them. This is a crazy and somewhat overwhelming environment and you will need them!

CAP UNITED AUDITIONS

CAP United Auditions in Atlanta, GA will offer seniors and Gap Year students the opportunity to audition for numerous outstanding performing arts programs around the nation, all in only 4 Days!

If you have any questions about the CAP United Auditions, please reach out to the CAP team today!

SCHOOLS

CAP has joined forces with some of the best performing arts colleges and universities in the nation to bring CAP United Auditions to life! We are thrilled to offer our amazing CAP students an invigorating and rewarding 4-day audition experience. We are excited about the schools that we have with us this year and can't wait for you to meet them and for them to meet you! In just 4 days you can audition for more schools than most students audition for in an entire college audition season. To see an updated list please visit www.capunitedauditions.com

AUDITIONS

During CAP UA you will have the opportunity to audition for all the CAP schools in attendance. The auditions take place on Friday and Saturday, with the schools being split in half with one half viewing auditions on Friday and the other half on Saturday. Each day starts off with vocal warmups then dance auditions. Each day will include a new choreographed dance routine, taught by our professional CAP choreographer. The CAP United Audition experience offers schools the opportunity to have callbacks with students they select during the audition process. These callbacks are a great way not only for the schools to gain more knowledge about the students but for the students to gain more personal knowledge about the schools and faculty. During the callbacks, you may be asked to do additional material or maybe just chat about yourself. You don't have to sacrifice the personal experience of an on-campus audition by attending these unified auditions!

AUDITION FORMAT & MATERIAL

1. MT Students will present 2 contrasting 16 bar songs and a 1-minute monologue. Acting students will present 1- 90 second monologue and 1- 16 bar song.

2. There will be a live accompanist for the main auditions on Friday and Saturday. Please bring music on a device for callback purposes.

3. Students will audition on both days. There will be a set group of colleges in attendance on Friday and another (separate) group of colleges attending the audition on Saturday. Colleges who audit the audition groups on Friday will have Friday afternoon/evening and Saturday call backs for the students they've requested to see or host workshops. Colleges who audit on Saturday will have Saturday afternoon/evening and Sunday morning to host callbacks or workshops.

4. Dance call will take place on a full dance floor (not carpet), if you are an experienced tapper bring tap shoes just in case!

Sample School Information

Before CAP UA you will receive a document with each school and their requirements listed. Below is a sample of what that will look like and what information will be included. Every school is different and so are their requirements!

STATE UNIVERSITY

- **AUDITION TYPE: First and Final**
- **AUDITOR**
  - Jane Doe
- **APPLICATION PROCESS:**
  - Students **DO NOT** have to apply academically to the university in order to be considered at CAP United Auditions. However, the will have to have the application completed **BEFORE** attending the callback on campus or at National Unifieds
- **PRE-SCREEN NEEDED PRIOR TO CAP UNITED: Yes**
  - All Students must apply to the program on GetAcceptd prior to **DEC 1**. This application will include pre-screen videos, an essay, headshot/resume.
- **CALLBACK PROCESS AT CAP UNITED**
  - Individual Callbacks
  - Callback material requirements: Two contrasting MT Songs, 32 bars (one contemporary/one traditional or standard) and a 16 bar pop rock song. Two 1-minute monologues contemporary realism preferred, no classical monologues.
  - Students we are interested in may be called back to the campus callback dates or given offers following CAP United. Some offers **MAY BE MADE** at CAP United.

CALLBACKS

If you get a callback from a live audition or a prescreen, then you know they are already interested in you. That's great! Now, prepare for those callbacks. Here are a few things to remember:

1. Be flexible!

Sometimes you may be asked to re-do one of your songs or monologues, we call this a "redirect". You may be asked to go through the material with a completely different energy or focus. These redirects are a good sign! It means they are interested in your work and want to see more. Once in a while, a redirect may seem extremely whacky, but go with it. Students have been asked, "Can you do that monologue again like a NYC bag lady?", "Can you do that again, but this time I want you to work off of our assistant," or, "Do that again but now you're going to do it as though you're talking in a library/across the street." Throw yourself into those redirects with 100% commitment. Be willing to take risks. A redirect is not about doing it "right" or "wrong". A redirect is about seeing how flexible, teachable, and committed you are as an actor. It is better to see someone fully invested in the material, than someone who is overly worried about being "right" and pulls back from making a strong choice. They can train an actor who makes big choices into an actor who makes better, big choices. They can do nothing with an actor who lives in their inhibitions and fears of being "wrong".

2. Be you!

Every college faculty wants to get to know who you are. They are not interested in seeing the "perfect" you or the version of you that you think they want to see. They want to see the real you, be it quirky, oddball, empathetic, or pensive. It's important that they get a real sense of who you are so they can determine if it's a good fit. It's an expensive and painful mistake to go to a college program that doesn't work well with your learning style, personality, financial needs and professional goals. To achieve a good fit, you've got to be authentic and honest. That doesn't mean you need to confess to all your weaknesses. It means dress like you would if you were going on a first date, but dress like you. Ask questions about the program that are important to you. Be willing to talk about some of your weaknesses, but be able to put a positive spin on that weakness. Have clearly defined goals for your future. They are not interested in perfect. They are interested in you.

3. Research the Program

Go online and look up the schools that have asked you to return for a callback. Look through their faculty page, alumni page and their curriculum. Take a few notes on their faculty achievements and the classes they teach. Is there anything there that peaks your interest or connects with your goals? Note the work that their alumni have done and be ready to connect that to your goals. The curriculum is hugely important! Do you want a program that emphasizes dance training? Are you looking for an emphasis on acting training or are you hoping for an evenly balanced program across all three disciplines of drama, dance and voice? Do you have any questions about how they approach their training? Write down two to three questions you have for the faculty and also write down three to five facts about the program that make you want to work with them. In other words, be ready to discuss their program and their people intelligently, as one who has done some research. The research generally takes about twenty to thirty minutes for each school and helps you represent yourself well in a callback.

WORKSHEET K
SAMPLE INTERVIEW QUESTIONS

⬚ What about our program makes it attractive to you and makes you want to come study with us?

⬚ What do you feel you have that would contribute to our program?

⬚ Where do you see yourself in 5 years? 10 years?

⬚ Tell me something about yourself.

⬚ Why do you want to be in theatre?

⬚ If you were never able to work in theatre again what would you see yourself doing?

> *This question is also asked in the following manner: If you could do anything else other than theatre what would you do?

> *If you could do one other thing with your life what would it be?

⬚ When you are cast in a role for a show, what process do you go through to get ready?

> *Also asked as: You are up for a big part – you have been given the script – How do you prepare?

⬚ Who inspired you?

⬚ What negative patterns get in the way of you being the best you can be?

⬚ Do you believe being an actor has a higher purpose – and if so what would you hope to contribute?

⬚ Why do you want to do this for a living?

⬚ Do you feel there are things you will need to sacrifice to be a good actor? What?

⬚ How do you feel about all the time and study it takes to be successful?

▪ What do you respect or admire in someone who has been successful in your business?

▪ Name your favorite performer/artist and why they are your favorite.

▪ What values do you hold as sacred that would not be compromised in your work?

▪ Who has influenced you to persist in this field?

▪ What do you think it takes to be successful as an actor/singer/dancer?

▪ What is your favorite part of being an actor/singer dancer?

▪ What do you feel you need to get stronger in order to be successful?

▪ What goals do you have for yourself this year?

▪ What distracts you or sabotages you from doing well?

▪ When your feedback is low to non-existent, where do you pull your strength from or is that when you give up on yourself?

▪ Describe yourself to me as an artist/performer?

▪ What qualities in you make you unique when coupled together?

▪ How do you feel about yourself?

▪ If you were describing yourself to someone as though you were not you but a friend of yours, how would you describe you?

▪ Specifically – what does it take to be a good actor?

▪ Why you?

▪ What contribution would you make to this class? A cast? A community? An audience?

▪ If you were an auditor, what would you be looking for?

▪ Besides talent, what makes you an artist?

▪ Looking at your present work ethic, patterns and skills, why didn't you get into a school you wanted?

▢ What artist/performer would you choose if you could have 24 hours with them? Why?

▢ What qualities and skills do you perceive it takes to be successful?

▢ You go to audition unprepared; how do you handle it?

▢ When did you first realize you wanted to do this?

▢ Do you believe you have what it takes to have a successful life in theatre or films?

▢ What is your ideal role?

▢ What type do you see yourself as? Who in theatre or films is that same or similar type?

▢ On a scale of 1-10 rate your skills as an:

* Actor

* Singer

* Dancer

▢ Would you consider yourself a risk taker?

▢ Do you consider yourself to have leadership qualities?

▢ What kind of college setting do you see yourself in?

Chapter Seven

AFTER THE AUDITIONS

THANK YOU NOTES

After each audition, take the time to send a thank you note to the faculty either via email or send a card through the mail. Make sure that you mention how much you appreciate their time and consideration. Point out the things about their program that you value and how much you enjoyed auditioning for them. Few students take the time for this small courtesy, but it helps the faculty remember you and adds to your professional reputation.

Sample Thank You Note

Dear Professor Theatre,

Thank you for the opportunity to audition for you and the rest of the faculty on November 14th. It was especially wonderful to learn more about your program and I appreciated the extra guidance that Sarah gave during the dance call. After this experience I am even more excited about State University and can say that it is at the top of my list.

I look forward to hearing for you soon!

Sincerely,

John Doe

MAKING A DECISION

If you have applied to several programs, marketed your type well, devoted yourself to training and auditioned well, the hope is that you will have multiple offers. The opportunity to make an informed choice between several programs raises your chance of attending the best program for you as a student. Choosing the right program is such an important decision simply because it affects you far beyond just four years of college. The relationships you build with faculty, the training you receive and the financial decisions you make in college will influence your professional life for years to come.

This process may feel like it is mimicking the start, when you were selecting schools for your list! The first thing you need do is sit down with your parents (or whoever is helping you financially) and decide what you can afford in tuition, housing, food, and extra expenses (there are always extra expenses especially as a theater major). Go over your FAFSA (Free Application for Federal Student Aid) and determine what, if any, loans and/or grants you qualify for. Reach out to the college programs who have offered you a spot and ask if there are any scholarships or work study programs that you could apply for to offset the cost of tuition. Every penny counts. If there is any school on the list that will put significant financial pressure on you or your family, you may want to take that school out of consideration. Taking out large loans will only mean that when you graduate those loans must be paid back with a monthly payment. If your loan payment is quite large, you will not have the resources you need to audition, continue training (it's lifelong, so prepare) and pay other bills. Most college graduates make very little, if anything, from their performance work for several years. It takes time to build the resume and reputation required to bring in money from performances. If you simply cannot afford the school, take it off your list of consideration.

Take into consideration how far the program is from home and add travel expenses to the financial expenses. Aside from the financial impact, some students simply don't want to be too far away from home. On the other hand, some students are anxious to move away and experience a new place.

After finances, the next important consideration is the curriculum. Forget about the name of the school and look at what they are going to teach you. Make a list of the classes for the degree without the name of the program being listed. Compare the lists with each other and see which one you are more excited about.

Talk to alumni and current students of the program. While you certainly cannot judge a program from just one student's opinion, you can get a fairly good idea of the culture within a program from talking to several of its current and former students. If distance or travel is not an issue, ask if you can tour the campus and sit in on a few classes. Take note of any concerns you have or any aspects of the experience that excite you.

Give greater consideration to programs that will challenge you as an artist. It's nice to be wanted, and attending a program that has actively recruited you can be a very good decision. However, also consider whether or not you are going to be the best one in a class. For example, if you want to be pushed in your dance skills, but you attend an Advanced Dance class on campus and it is too easy for you that may be a concern. Being the best in the room is not a good thing. You need to have other incredibly talented artists around you who are going to inspire and motivate you to grow.

DID YOU KNOW…

The CAP website has a feature to help you compare the schools that you have offers from!

Need help choosing the right school?
Get a consult with a CAP Coach!

WORKSHEET L

SCHOOL COMPARISON SHEET

School 1	School 2
Total Cost:	Total Cost:
Scholarship $:	Scholarship $:
Senior Showcase: Yes No	Senior Showcase: Yes No
Private Voice: Yes No Group	Private Voice: Yes No Group
Vocal Styles:	Vocal Styles:
# of Dance Classes:	# of Dance Classes:
Dance Styles:	
Acting Styles:	Acting Styles:
Total Major Credits:	Total Major Credits:
How Far From Home:	How Far From Home:
Can you have a car?	Can you have a car?
Cast Freshman Year? Yes No	Cast Freshman Year? Yes No
What do you like the most?	What do you like the most?:
What do you wish they had?:	What do you wish they had?:

GAP YEAR

We most commonly see GAP students that fit in one of two categories. The first is a student that wanted a traditional senior year of high school and did not go through the college audition process but has instead decided to take a Gap year to devote to this process. The second, is a student that may have gone through the college audition process during their senior year but did not find the success they were hoping for during the process.

A performing arts Gap year is a year of intense technical training following high school graduation. Instructors may suggest a Gap year for a student who has struggled to train during a busy high school career and does not feel adequately prepared for college auditions in the performing arts.

Focusing on intensive training for a Gap year can greatly improve your results at college auditions and provides a better technical foundation for you to draw from during your college career. Ideally, a Gap year student will begin their year of intense training immediately following high school graduation and throughout the summer. While we use the term Gap "year", college auditions and the pre-screen deadlines begin in late Fall, which means that Gap year students only have months to train before beginning the audition process. Summer training gives you the benefit of two additional months of training before the audition process begins.

After college auditions are completed, Gap year students remain focused on training, but may then broaden their training to include other aspects of the performing arts that will benefit them in their college program (i.e. music theory, repertoire, script analysis, choreography, etc.), depending on the individual needs of each student.

The purpose of the Gap year is:

1. To focus on your technical training, thereby improving the results of college auditions
2. To prepare for the rigorous demands of a college training program.

During a student's GAP year they may take core college classes from a local school or online but it should be noted that their main focus should remain on their arts training and having the best result during the audition season.

The CAP Gap year students have enjoyed remarkable success in their audition process. Many of our Gap year students have been accepted into prestigious programs around the world. Keep in mind that a Gap year is not recommended for every student. The faculty at CAP can help parents and students evaluate if a Gap year is an option they should pursue.

GAP YEAR DO's & DON'Ts

Remember, the purpose of a gap year is for a student to truly focus on training without having to focus on school grades. If you reach the end of your senior year, and you feel that you did not accomplish your goals, you can take a gap year and audition again the following year. You can also take a gap year if you need to raise your test scores or get a few college classes under your belt. With that said, the MAIN goal of a gap year is to TRAIN, TRAIN, TRAIN. It will not help you if you do not give your all to that year. Here is a list of a few do's and do not's for your gap year.

Do:

Take General Education classes at a local college or online, so that you will have time in your college schedule for extra classes.

Get a part time job to set aside some money. This will help you with expenses when you are at school.

Take every dance class you can find. Seek private acting and vocal coaches, if you have not done so already. Training should be your main goal during that gap year.

Set small goals to give yourself a sense of accomplishment.

Take the SAT and ACT again. The higher the score, the more scholarship money you will be eligible to receive.

Volunteer for local charities to boost your application value.

Don't:

Enroll in a local college and become a full-time student with a large course load. Remember that some credits may not transfer and your goal is to get ready for the College Audition process. Don't waste your time and money on classes and courses that will not help you in the long run!

Get a full-time job. It is imperative that you train as much as is possible.

Audition for local shows that will interfere with your training.

Rest on your achievements. Remember you are seeking excellence.

Lock into one school or program. Try to get a feel for what you like by visiting local schools.

Become so busy that you forget what you are trying to accomplish.

Chapter Eight

BEFORE YOU GO TO COLLEGE

Once you've made your decision and committed in writing to a program, the real work begins. Yes, believe it or not, getting into a program is the easy part. Staying in and thriving in a program is the hard part.

Here are two things to consider as you approach your Freshman year of college:

1. Continue with your training. Most programs will ask their Freshmen to audition within the first two weeks of classes. For some programs, this audition is simply for the whole faculty to evaluate you and place you within classes or with private instructors. For other programs, this audition is for the upcoming season of shows. Either way, you need to show that you have improved and grown since they saw you at your initial audition or callback. If you haven't improved, that could be a red flag to faculty that maybe you're not a worker. That's not the impression you want to make. Show up to your Freshman audition ready to set your reputation as a motivated and growing artist.

2. Your first set of professional auditions for summer work, etc. will require prescreens (either via video or your college faculty) towards the end of your first semester of college. These auditions will be offered through your regional theater conference (Google it for your region), UPTA, A1, etc. You may be overwhelmed with the schedule and demands of a college theater program, so have some material that you are solid with before you even step on campus. Have several songs to choose from that you can use for those prescreens, as well as several monologues that are one minute in length. If you are prepared with this material, getting those prescreens completed for your first professional auditions will be a lot easier and more successful. It is important to book work during the summer of each school year and/or complete an internship, because you have to completely rebuild your resume once you start college and that takes time and experience.

The exciting thing is that you have made it through the college audition process. You should be SO proud of yourself and the journey you have been on over the last year. Reflect on the experiences you have had, auditioning for multiple schools and faculty members. You are a part of this amazing performing arts community, continue to push yourself and grow. Take advantage of every experience that comes your way during your collegiate experience. You are going to grow more during the next 4 years than you even thought possible, you are going to be stretched and molded into a remarkable artist and we couldn't be MORE excited for you!

Thank you for letting us be a part of your journey!

School List

There are MANY amazing programs around the world that offer Acting and Musical Theatre training at the collegiate level. Below is a list of schools that we have frequently had students audition for during their college audition process. There are new programs popping up all the time, so do your research and find the schools that fit you. Hopefully, this will at least give you a starting point in creating your list!

Abilene Christian University

AMDA

Arizona State University

Auburn University

Baldwin Wallace

Ball State University

Baylor University

Belhaven University

Belmont University

Birmingham-Southern University

Boston Conservatory

Boston University

Brenau University

Brigham Young University

Bristol Old Vic Theatre School

California Institute of the Arts

Carnegie Mellon University

Coastal Carolina University

College of Charleston

Colorado Mesa University

Columbus State University

Cornish College of the Arts

Dean College

DePaul University

Drake University

Drama Center London

East Carolina University

Elon University

Emerson University

Emory and Henry University

Five Towns College

Florida Southern College

Florida State University

Guildhall School of Music & Drama

Illinois Wesleyan University

Indiana University-Bloomington

Ithaca University

Jacksonville University

James Madison University

Julliard

Kennesaw State University

Kent State University

Liverpool Institute of Performing Arts

London Academy of Music & Dramatic Art

Long Island University- Post

Loyola Marymount University

Lynn University

Manhattan School of Music

Marymount Manhattan College

Millikin University

Missouri State University

Molloy College

Montclair University

Mountview Academy of Theatre Arts

Muhlenberg College

Nebraska Wesleyan University

New Mexico State University

Niagara University

NYU Steinhardt

NYU Tisch School of the Arts

Ohio Northern University

Ohio University

Oklahoma City University

Otterbein University

Ouachita Baptist University

Pace University

Pennsylvania State University

Pepperdine University

Point Park University

Rider University

Roosevelt University

Royal Academy of Dramatic Art

Royal Central School of Speech & Drama

Royal Conservatoire of Scotland

Royal Welsh College of Music & Drama

Rutgers University

Sam Houston State University

San Diego State University

Sarah Lawrence College

Savannah College of Art and Design

Shenandoah University

Southern Methodist University

SUNY Purchase

Syracuse University

Temple University

Texas Christian University

Texas State University

Texas Tech University

The New School for Drama

University of Alabama

University of Alabama- Birmingham

University of Arizona

University of California-Irvine

University of Central Florida

University of Central Oklahoma

University of Chicago

University of Cincinnati College-Conservatory of Music

University of Evansville

University of Florida

University of Hartford

University of Memphis

University of Miami

University of Michigan

University of Minnesota

University of Minnesota-Duluth

University of Montevallo

University of New Hampshire

University of North Carolina School of the Arts

University of Northern Colorado

University of Oklahoma

University of Tampa

University of Texas -El Paso

University of the Arts

University of Utah

University of West Florida

University of West Georgia

University of Wisconsin -Stevens Point

Valdosta State University

Viterbo University

Wagner College

Wester University

Western Carolina University

Western Michigan University

Wichita State University

Wright State University

Overused Material

One of the most important parts of your College Audition journey is choosing your audition material. This task can seem impossible at times. You will want to make certain the material you have chosen is not overdone, overused, or really popular. We have compiled a short list of material to stay away from as well as some tips to help you stay away from pieces faculty may see too often. Overdone material is not "bad" material, on the contrary, usually it is good material. That is why it is overdone. So, if you have a song or monologue from the list below, keep it in your rep book, just don't include it in your initial audition package or prescreens.

VOCAL SELECTIONS

SHOWS TO STAY AWAY FROM

* Anything currently on Broadway, this includes Revivals
* Anything that just left Broadway or might be on a National Tour
* Popular or Iconic shows: Sound of Music, Les Misérables, Phantom of the Opera, RENT, Grease…. you get the picture!
* Popular shows produced in schools and youth theatres- Legally Blonde, Seussical, Addams Family, Shrek, You're A Goodman Charlie Brown…. again, you get the picture!
* Disney…. unless they ask for a Disney song, just stay away from Disney as your initial package pieces

* Risqué Topics-think Heathers, Avenue Q, Spring Awakening, Book of Mormon
* Songs that appear in a Singer's Anthology book, these are some great songs, it is just that everyone has these books so you run the chance of them having been done…. A LOT!

OVERUSED FEMALE SONGS

"Adelaide's Lament" from Guys & Dolls
"All That Jazz" from Chicago
"Astonishing" from Little Women
"Big Spender" from Sweet Charity
"Breathe" from In The Heights
"Castle on A Cloud" from Les Misérables
"Defying Gravity" from Wicked
"Don't Rain on My Parade" from Funny Girl
"For Good" from Wicked
"Gimme Gimme" from Thoroughly Modern Millie
"Good Morning Baltimore" from Hairspray
"Gorgeous" from Apple Tree
"I Could Have Danced All Night" from My Fair Lady
"I Dreamed a Dream" from Les Misérables
"I Hate Men" from Kiss Me Kate
"I'm the Greatest Star" from Funny Girl
"If I Loved You" from Carousel
"In My Own Little Corner" From Cinderella
"It's A Privilege to Pee" from Urinetown
"Live Out Loud" from A Little Princess
"Mama Who Bore Me" from Spring Awakening
"Maybe" from Annie
"Memory" from Cats
"Much More" from The Fantasticks
"Not For the Life of Me" from Thoroughly Modern Millie

"Not While I'm Around" from Sweeney Todd
"On My Own" from Les Misérables
"One Perfect Moment" from Bring It On
"Popular" from Wicked
"Pretty Funny" from Dogfight
"Pulled" from Addams Family
"Screwloose" From Cry Baby
"Shy" from Once Upon A Mattress
"Somewhere Over the Rainbow" from The Wizard of Oz
"Spark of Creation" from Children of Eden
"Still Hurting" from The Last Five Years
"Stranger to the Rain" from Children of Eden
"Suddenly Seymour" from Little Shop of Horrors
"Summertime" from Porgy & Bess
"Vanilla Ice Cream" from She Loves Me
"Watch What Happens" from Newsies

OVERUSED MALE SONGS

"Aldolfo" from Drowsy Chaperone
"Anthem" from Chess
"Any Dream Will Do" From Joseph…..Dreamcoat
"Being Alive" from Company
"Bring Him Home" from Les Misérables
"Close Every Door" from Joseph
"Corner of the Sky" from Pippin
"Empty Chairs" from Les Misérables
"Friend Like Me" from Aladdin
"Giants in the Sky" from Into The Woods
"I Believe" from Book of Mormon
"I Can Go The Distance" from Hercules
"I'll Cover You" from Rent
"I'm Alive" from Next to Normal
"If I Loved You" from Carousel

"It All Fades Away" from Bridges of Madison County
"Johanna" from Sweeney Todd
"Laura,Laura" from High Fidelity
"Lost in the Wilderness" from Children of Eden
"Luck Be A Lady" From Guys and Dolls
"Memphis Lives in Me" from Memphis
"Mr. Cellophane" from Chicago
"Proud of Your Boy" from Aladdin
"Purpose" from Avenue Q
"Santa Fe" from Newsies
"Santa Fe" from Rent
"Springtime For Hitler" from The Producers
"Take A Chance on Me" from Little Women
"This is The Moment" from Jekyll and Hyde
"Who I'd Be" from Shrek
"Willkomen" from Cabaret
"Wondering" from Bridges of Madison County

MONOLOGUE SELECTIONS

Overdone monologues are a little trickier than overdone vocal selections. While there are not as many to specifically list, we do have some tips to help you pick monologues that are not as used and haven't been heard by every college faculty member across the world!

SHOWS TO STAY AWAY FROM

* Classics American Theatre such as "Crucible", "Our Town", "Glass Menagerie", anything by Neil Simon…. good stuff but it has been around forever and we all know these by heart.

* Popular shows produced by schools- "She Kills Monsters", "Almost Maine", "Radium Girls", "Peter and the Starcatcher"...you get the picture!
* Monologues from TV and Film
* Monologues from Musicals...think Luisa's speech before "Much More"
* Monologues with risqué or crude material... you don't need to add a shock factor to your selections!
* Anything written by Christopher Durang, not only because of some subject matter, but also because they are widely popular!

OVERUSED FEMALE MONOLOGUES

A Streetcar Named Desire - *"I loved someone, too, and the person I loved I lost. He was..."*

An Ideal Husband - *"Well, Tommy has proposed to me again..."*

And Turning, Stay - *"Don't you dare walk away from me! And don't tell me you're sorry!"*

Brighton Beach Memoirs -*"Oh, God, he was so handsome. Always dressed so dapper..."*

Fat Men in Skirts - *"I am Popo Martin. My friends call me Popo Martin."*

For Colored Girls....-*ALL*

Goodbye Charles - *"The Divorce Papers"* monologue

Gruesome Playground Injuries- *"You can't marry that girl, Doug..."*

House of Blue Leaves-*" I won't cook for you til you marry me..."*

Picasso at the Lapin Agile -*"it was about two weeks ago..."*

Proof - *"I lived with him. I spent my life with him. I fed him..."*

Quilters-*Sunbonnet Sue*

Rabbit Hole - *"Do you really not know me, Howie? Do you really not know how utterly..."*

Scuba Lessons-*"Did you ever wake up and know it was going to be your day?"*

Slow Dance on the Killing Ground-*Losing virginity speech*

The Fifth of July - *"I'm going to be the greatest artist Missouri has ever produced.."*

The Star Spangled Girl - *"Mr. Cornell, I have tried to be neighborly. I have tried to be ..."*

Valhalla-*Feelings for James Avery*

Wonder of the World- *Barbie Head Monologue*

OVERUSED MALE MONOLOGUES

4000 Miles- *Chicken crash monologue*

Aloha Say the Pretty Girls- *ALL*

Biloxi Blues- *"I was in the latrine alone..."*

Boys' Life - *"I would have destroyed myself for this woman..."*

Danny and the Deep Blue Sea -*"I was at this party. A guy named Skull..."*

Danny and the Deep Blue Sea-*All of Danny's monologues*

Fat Pig - *"I'm weak. That's what I basically learned from our time together"*

I Hate Hamlet- *"Last night, right from the start, I knew I was bombing..."*

I Never Sang for my Father-*"That night I left my father's house…"*

Mass Appeal-*Dead goldfish speech*

Nourish the Beast- *"I don't know how old I was when they put me in the orphanage..."*

Pterodactyls- *"In the beginning, there were dinosaurs..."*

Rabbit Hole -*"So, I don't see any photos anywhere. The one in the article was nice..."*

Raised in Captivity- *Mr. Giggles the Clown*

Rosencrantz & Guildenstern are Dead- *"Do you ever think of yourself as actually dead..."*

Shape of Things- *"This isn't art"*

Suburbia- *about moving to New York City*

Take Me Out- *"I've been watching baseball nonstop since the day I was told you were ..."*

The Laramie Project -*"I've lived in Wyoming my whole life. The family has been in ..."*

College Audition Project

THE CAP WEBSITE

If, while going through this book, you wish you had some extra help, consider becoming a CAP student and getting access to the CAP Website and the Navigator.

The Navigator is an online tool that can help with everything from school selections to scheduling, with the capability to send reminders about upcoming auditions and deadlines. You can store your media files and even share your information with parents and teachers. Plus, everything you love about this book can be found digitally on your online account!

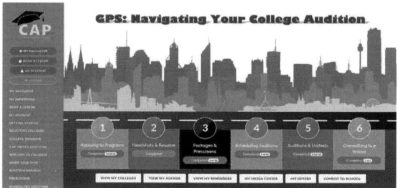

THE CAP APP

Yes, we are mobile! We know that most of you live your life on the go and it is not always easy to get to a desktop computer or even a laptop. We also know that you NEVER go anywhere without your phone. So, we took everything on our online site and put it in an app. You can access CAP and your Navigator on any mobile device, Apple or Android.

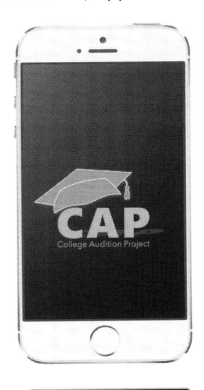

CAP UNITED AUDITIONS

PLUS....by being a CAP student you are eligible to register to attend CAP United Auditions!

These private unified auditions are only open to CAP students and host some of the best schools around. Students will have the opportunity to audition for EVERY school in attendance, no need to pick and choose!

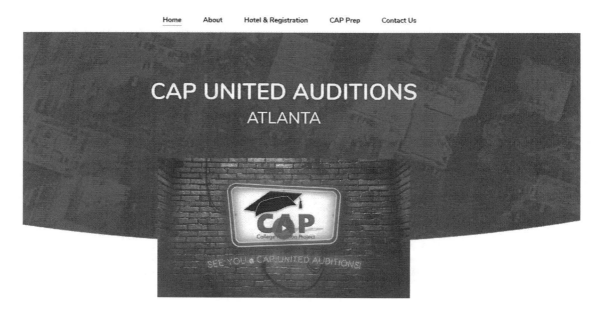

CAP PREP

Are you a rising Sophomore or Junior?

You might want to look at our CAP Prep program. This 2 day intensive takes place during our CAP United Auditions in Atlanta, GA. During the 2 days, students will have the opportunity to take amazing workshops from college faculty, industry professionals and the CAP team.

To Register for the CAP Website: www.collegeauditionproject.com

To Register for CAP UA or CAP Prep: www.capunitedauditions.com

Author's Bios

Dave Clemmons

Headshot by Marcigliano Photography

Dave Clemmons has been in the college audition coaching business long before college audition coaching was even a thing. His extensive career both in front and behind the casting table has positioned him to be an ultimate source of information for those going through the college audition process. As a performer, he spent time on Broadway in such shows as *The Scarlet Pimpernel* and *Les Misérables* and his National Tour credits include *Les Misérables*, *Jekyll & Hyde* and *Whistle Down The Wind* as well as numerous other National and Regional credits. Dave spent 15+ years behind the table as a Producer and Casting Director, most notably with *Dave Clemmons Casting*, where he cast more than 100 Broadway, Off-Broadway, National Tours, Workshops and Regional Productions. Over the last 20+ years, Dave has spent time traveling as a guest artist and lecturer to some of the top training programs around the nation, teaching workshops and developing relationships with top faculty and industry professionals. Dave is also a founder and permanent faulty member for *The Performing Arts Project*, where he shares his vast knowledge of the industry and the college audition process with students during the summer. In 2009, Dave started the *Dave Clemmons College Advisory Program* (D.C.C.A.P), where he has been coaching students through their college audition journeys for the last decade. To find out more about Dave visit https://www.ibdb.com/broadway-cast-staff/dave-clemmons-35590

Michelle Evans

Headshot by Jake Pearce Photography

Michelle is the owner of MJE Acting Studio where she offers her services as a private acting, audition, and college audition coach to students both in the US and abroad through online lessons. Michelle has been working professionally since 2004, both on and off the stage, as an actress, director and teaching artist. She has won several awards for her directorial work both on regional and national levels. As a private acting coach, Michelle's students have had success finding entrance into top universities as well as professionally on Broadway, National Tours, Regional Theatre and TV/Film. Michelle is a frequent guest artist and IE Judge for Thespian festivals around the US, local high schools and theatre companies. In addition, Michelle has served as an adjudicator and committee member for the Shuler Awards in Atlanta (2012-2018), Kansas City's Blue Star Awards (2019-present), as well as One Act, Speech & Debate, and Literary competitions around the nation. Always in pursuit of sharing her knowledge with others, in 2017, Michelle began her writing adventures. You can find her articles and columns on www.performerstuff.com and www.theatreartlife.com. Michelle loves working alongside her CAP colleagues and coaching the CAP students through all of their acting needs. You can find out more about Michelle at www.mjeactingstudio.com!

Holly Garmon

Headshot by Marcigliano Photography

Holly is the owner and founder of The Performer's Warehouse in Alpharetta, GA where she helped bring together one of the first and finest teams in Atlanta whose sole focus was helping students prepare for their college auditions. Through this team Holly helped to develop the P3 Conservatory at Performer's Warehouse, a daytime conservatory for Musical Theatre hopefuls, in which students were able to give equal attention to their acting, voice and dance skills allowing them to develop all three disciplines in detail. While teaching is one of her passions, Holly also founded Performer's Warehouse Productions and produced several shows with Dave Clemmons, including Les Misérables, allowing high school and college students the opportunity to work together with current professionals on the award-winning Alliance stage. Holly was born and graduated high school in New Orleans. She went on to Mississippi College where she graduated cum laude with a BA in English and a double major in Business Management. She is the mother of three children who have gone on to work professionally in the performing and visual arts fields. Her former students can be found on Broadway, National Tours, Regional Theatres throughout the US and in top theatre training programs all over the world such as Royal Welsh, Royal Scotland, CCM, Texas State, Otterbein, BYU, University of Alabama, Coastal Carolina, Cal Arts, and Texas Christian to name a few.

Camiah Mingorance

Headshot by Marcigliano Photography

Camiah has been singing and performing professionally for years, including tours, Atlanta theatre and private events. She has taught voice, theatre and music since 1996 and has had the honor of music directing for the renowned Dave Clemmons, as well as for Atlanta theatre companies. Camiah is honored to be the official voice teacher for the award-winning Aurora Theater in Lawrenceville, Georgia. Her passion for developing healthy voices and guiding singers towards successful professional careers has driven her to study with some of the world's most respected vocal scientists and researchers, including Dr. Ingo Titze, along with doctors, speech language pathologists and other respected voice specialists. She is a Mentor Teacher for Vocology in Practice and International Voice Teachers of Mix and frequently writes educational articles for their worldwide communities of accomplished voice teachers. Camiah is a proud voting member of Pan American Vocology Association, where she strives to keep her vocal training on the cutting edge of research. Her students can be found on Broadway, on National Tours and in the world's leading musical theatre college programs, from Royal Conservatoire of Scotland to Cincinnati Conservatory of Music, from Berkley College of Music to Otterbein University. Her students excel in musical theatre, music therapy, vocal performance and song writing.

Pat Valleroy

Headshot by Marcigliano Photography

Pat lives in Atlanta with her husband John, and their three adult children. She specializes in the college audition process, and in helping high school students reach their potential. She has worked in Theatre for many years, as a teacher, director, managing director, and artistic director. In 2011, she began to help guide students through the maze of the audition world. After seeing the difficulty firsthand when her son went to college for musical theatre, she realized there had to be a better way. She went to work for The Performer's Warehouse, where she found her home. As the college program evolved and changed, she was able to help guide many students through this process. She taught the Senior Audition class at The Performer's Warehouse, where she specialized in the application process, school lists, headshots, resumes, and audition questions. In 2017, CAP was formed as the team realized that students across the world needed help navigating through this process. Pat has helped students get into many of the best theatre programs in the country, and in Europe. She loves to work with universities, students, and families as they embark on this journey. She stresses to all that you will get into the program you are supposed to get into, and to remember that you will get out of a program what you put into it. She looks forward to working with you!

Notes

NOTES:_____

_____
_____
_____
_____
_____
_____
_____
_____
_____
_____
_____
_____
_____
_____
_____
_____
_____
_____
_____
_____
_____
_____
_____
_____
_____
_____
_____
_____
_____
_____
_____
_____

NOTES:_____

_____
_____
_____
_____
_____
_____
_____
_____
_____
_____
_____
_____
_____
_____
_____
_____
_____
_____
_____
_____
_____
_____
_____
_____
_____
_____
_____
_____
_____
_____
_____

Made in the USA
Columbia, SC
25 September 2019